W9-BPM-023

Rick Steves'
ITALIAN
Phrase Book & Dictionary

4th Edition

AVALON
TRAVEL

Thanks to the team of people at *Europe Through the Back Door*
who helped make this book possible: Mary Carlson, Dave
Hoerlein, Mary Romano, and . . .

Italian translation: Giulia Fiorini and Alessandra Panieri
Italian proofreading: Manfredo Guerzoni
Phonetics: Risa Laib
Layout: Rich Sorensen and Colleen Murphy
Maps: David C. Hoerlein

Edited by Risa Laib and Rich Sorensen

Avalon Travel Publishing
1400 65th Street, Suite 250, Emeryville, CA 94608
formerly published by John Muir Publications

Copyright © 1999, 1996, 1995, 1993 by Rick Steves
Cover copyright © 1999 by John Muir Publications
All rights reserved.

Printed in the U.S.A. by Banta Company
Fourth edition. Eighth printing July 2002.

ISBN 1-56261-478-9

Cover photos: Colosseum, Rome, Italy; © Blaine Harrington III
            Foreground photo: © Blaine Harrington III

Distributed to the book trade by
Publishers Group West
Berkeley, California

*While every effort has been made to keep the content of this
book accurate, the author and publisher accept no responsibility
whatsoever for anyone ordering bad beer or getting messed up in
any other way because of the linguistic confidence this phrase
book has given them.*

To get the most out of this book, take the time to internalize and put into practice my Italian pronunciation tips. Remember that Italians, more than their European neighbors, are forgiving of your linguistic fumbling. Don't worry too much about memorizing grammatical rules, like which gender a particular noun is—the important thing is to rise above sex . . . and communicate!

This book has a dictionary and a nifty menu decoder. You'll also find Italian telephone tips and a handy tear-out "cheat sheet." Tear it out and keep it in your pocket, so you can easily use it to memorize key phrases during idle moments. As you prepare for your trip, you may want to read this year's edition of my *Rick Steves' Italy* guidebook.

Italy can be the most intense, difficult and rewarding destination in Europe. Travelers either love it—or they quickly see the big sights and flee to Switzerland. To me, someone's love of Italy is a sign of a good traveler—thoughtful, confident, and extroverted. If this phrase book helps make that happen, or if you have suggestions for making it better, I'd love to hear from you. I personally read and value all feedback. My address is Europe Through the Back Door, P.O. Box 2009, Edmonds, WA 98020, tel. 425/771-8303, fax 425/771-0833, e-mail: rick@ricksteves.com.

Happy travels, and *buona fortuna* (good luck) as you hurdle the language barrier!

Rick Steves

Phoning, E-mail, Post Office, & Red Tape

- Phoning 102
- E-mail 103
- Post Office 105
- Red tape & profanity 108

Help! 110
- Help for women 111

Health 112
- Contacts, glasses, and toiletries 115

Chatting
- Who's who 118
- Family and work 118
- Chatting with children 119
- Favorite things 121
- Thanks a million 122
- Travel talk and map musings 123
- Create your own conversation 127
- Weather 131
- An Italian romance 131
- Conversing with Italian animals 134

Appendix:
English-Italian Dictionary 135
Italian-English Dictionary 153
Hurdling the Language Barrier 171
Let's Talk Telephones 174
Tear-Out Cheat Sheet 177
Faxing your hotel reservation 179

Maps
- Major rail lines in Italy 27
- Italy 125
- U.S.A and Europe 126

Hi, I'm Rick Steves.

I'm the only mono-lingual speaker I know who's had the nerve to design a series of European phrase books. But that's one of the things that makes them better. You see, after 25 summers of travel through Europe, I've learned first-hand (1) what's essential for communication in another country, and (2) what's not. I've assembled these important words and phrases in a logical, no-frills format, and I've worked with native Europeans and seasoned travelers to give you the simplest, clearest translations possible.

But this book is more than just a pocket translator. The words and phrases have been carefully selected to help you have a smarter, smoother trip in my favorite country without going broke. Italy used to be cheap and chaotic. These days it's neither. It's better organized than ever—and often more expensive than France or Germany. The key to getting more out of every travel dollar is to get closer to the local people, and to rely less on entertainment, restaurants, and hotels that cater only to foreign tourists. This book will not only help you order a meal at a locals-only Venetian restaurant—it'll help you talk to the family that runs the place . . . about their kids, social issues, travel dreams, and favorite flavors of *gelati*. Long after your memories of museums have faded, you'll still treasure the personal encounters you had with your new Italian friends.

A good phrase book should help you enjoy your Italian experience—not just survive it—so I've added a healthy dose of humor. But please use these phrases carefully, in a self-effacing spirit. Remember that one ugly American can undo the goodwill built by dozens of culturally-sensitive ones.

Contents

Getting Started 1
Italian Basics 4
● Survival phrases 5
● Alphabet 11
Numbers, Money, & Time
● Numbers 14
● Money 17
● Time 18
Transportation
● Trains 22
● Buses and subways 29
● Taxis 31
● Rental wheels 33
● Driving 34
● Finding your way 37
Sleeping
● Places to stay and reserving a room 41
● Checking out 49
● Camping 50
● Laundry 50
Eating
● Restaurants 53
● Drinking 76
● Picnicking 82
● Italian-English menu decoder 84
Sightseeing, Shopping, & Entertainment
● Sightseeing 89
   Discounts 90
● Shopping 95
   Repair 99
● Entertainment 100

Avalon Travel Publishing guidebooks by Rick Steves

Europe 101: History and Art for the Traveler (with Gene
   Openshaw)
*Rick Steves' Mona Winks: Self-guided Tours of Europe's Top
   Museums* (with Gene Openshaw)
Rick Steves' Postcards from Europe
Rick Steves' Best of Europe
Rick Steves' Europe Through the Back Door
Rick Steves' France, Belgium & the Netherlands (with Steve
   Smith)
Rick Steves' Germany, Austria & Switzerland
Rick Steves' Great Britain & Ireland
Rick Steves' Italy
Rick Steves' Russia & the Baltics (with Ian Watson)
Rick Steves' Scandinavia
Rick Steves' Spain & Portugal
Rick Steves' London (with Gene Openshaw)
Rick Steves' Paris (with Steve Smith and Gene Openshaw)
Rick Steves' Phrase Books for: French, German, Italian,
   Spanish/Portuguese, and French/Italian/German
Asia Through the Back Door

Rick Steves' company, *Europe Through the Back Door*,
provides many services for budget travelers, including a free
quarterly newsletter/catalog, budget travel books and accessories, Eurailpasses (with free video and travel advice included),
free-spirited European tours, on-line travel tips, and a Travel
Resource Center in Edmonds, WA. For a free newsletter, call,
write, or e-mail:

Europe Through the Back Door
120 Fourth Avenue N., Box 2009
Edmonds, WA 98020 USA
Tel: 425/771-8303, Fax: 425/771-0833
Web: http://www.ricksteves.com

GETTING STARTED

Getting Started

User-friendly Italian
...is easy to get the hang of. Some Italian words are so familiar, you'd think they were English. If you can say *pizza, lasagna,* and *spaghetti,* you can speak Italian.

There are a few unusual twists to its pronunciation:

C usually sounds like C in cat.
   But *C* followed by *E* or *I* sounds like CH in chance.
CH sounds like C in cat.
E often sounds like AY in play.
G usually sounds like G in get.
   But *G* followed by *E* or *I* sounds like G in gentle.
GH sounds like G in *spaghetti.*
GLI sounds like LI in million. The G is silent.
GN sounds like GN in *lasagna.*
H is never pronounced.
I sounds like EE in seed.
R is rolled as in *brrravo!*
SC usually sounds like SK in skip.
   But *SC* followed by *E* or *I* sounds like SH in shape.
Z usually sounds like TS in hits, and sometimes like the
   sound of DZ in kids.

Have you ever noticed that most Italian words end in a vowel? It's *o* if the word is masculine and *a* if it's feminine. So a *bambino* gets blue and a *bambina* gets pink. A man is *generoso* (generous), a woman is *generosa*. A man will say, *"Sono sposato"* (I am married). A woman will say, *"Sono sposata.*" In this book, we show gender-bender words like this: *generoso[a]*. If you are speaking of a woman (which includes women speaking about themselves), use the *a* ending. It's always pronounced "ah." If a noun or adjective ends in *e*, such as *cantante* (singer) or *gentile* (kind), the same word applies to either sex.

Adjective endings agree with the noun. It's *cara amica* (a dear female friend) and *caro amico* (a dear male friend). Sometimes the adjective comes after the noun, as in *vino rosso* (red wine).

Plurals are formed by changing the final letter of the noun: *a* becomes *e*, and *o* becomes *i*. So it's one *pizza* and two *pizze*, and one cup of *cappuccino* and two cups of *cappuccini*.

Italians usually pronounce every letter in a word, so *due* (two) is **doo**-ay. Sometimes two vowels share one syllable. *Piano* sounds like peeah-noh. The "peeah" is one syllable. When one vowel in a pair should be emphasized, it will appear in bold letters: *italiano* is ee-tah-lee**ah**-noh.

The key to Italian inflection is to remember this simple rule: most Italian words have their accent on the second-to-last syllable. To override this rule, Italians sometimes insert an accent: *città* (city) is pronounced chee-**tah**.

Italians are animated. You may think two Italians are arguing when in reality they're agreeing enthusiastically. When they do argue, it's fast and furious! Body language is a very important part of communicating in Italy—especially hand gestures (see Gestures for details). Watch and imitate. Be confident, and have fun communicating in Italian. The Italians really do want to understand you, and are forgiving of a yankee-fied version of their language.

Here's a quick guide to the phonetics we've used in this book:

ah	like A in father.
ay	like AY in play.
eh	like E in let.
ee	like EE in seed.
ehr	sounds like "air."
g	like G in go.
o	like O in cost.
oh	like O in note.
oo	like OO in too.
or	like OR in core.
ow	like OW in cow.
s	like S in sun.
ts	like TS in hits. It's a small explosive sound. Think of *pizza* (pee-tsah).

Italian Basics

Greeting and meeting Italians:

Good day.	**Buon giorno.**	bwohn **jor**-noh
Good morning.	**Buon giorno.**	bwohn **jor**-noh
Good evening.	**Buona sera.**	**bwoh**-nah **say**-rah
Good night.	**Buona notte.**	**bwoh**-nah **not**-tay
Hi / Bye. (informal)	**Ciao.**	chow
Mr.	**Signore**	seen-**yor**-ay
Mrs.	**Signora**	seen-**yoh**-rah
Miss	**Signorina**	seen-yoh-**ree**-nah
How are you?	**Come sta?**	**koh**-may stah
Very well, thanks.	**Molto bene,**	**mohl**-toh **behn**-ay
	grazie.	**graht**-seeay
And you?	**E lei?**	ay lehee
My name is...	**Mi chiamo...**	mee kee**ah**-moh
What's your name?	**Come si chiama?**	**koh**-may see keeah-mah
Pleased to meet you.	**Piacere.**	peeah-**chay**-ray
Where are you from?	**Di dove è?**	dee **doh**-vay eh
I am / Are you...?	**Sono / È...?**	**soh**-noh / eh
...on vacation	**...in vacanza**	een vah-**kahnt**-sah
...on business	**...qui per lavoro**	kwee pehr lah-**voh**-roh
See you later.	**A più tardi.**	ah pew **tar**-dee
Goodbye.	**Arrivederci.**	ah-ree-vay-**dehr**-chee
Good luck!	**Buona fortuna!**	**bwoh**-nah for-**too**-nah
Have a good trip!	**Buon viaggio!**	bwohn vee**ah**-joh

The greeting *"Buon giorno"* (Good day) turns to *"Buona sera"* (Good evening) in the late afternoon.

Survival phrases

In 800, Charlemagne traveled to Rome and became the Holy Roman Emperor using only these phrases. They are repeated on your tear-out cheat sheet later in this book.

The essentials:

Good day.	**Buon giorno.**	bwohn **jor**-noh
Do you speak English?	**Parla inglese?**	**par**-lah een-**glay**-zay
Yes. / No.	**Sì. / No.**	see / noh
I don't speak Italian.	**Non parlo l'italiano.**	nohn **par**-loh lee-tah-leeah-noh
I'm sorry.	**Mi dispiace.**	mee dee-speeah-chay
Please.	**Per favore.**	pehr fah-**voh**-ray
Thank you.	**Grazie.**	**graht**-seeay
It's (not) a problem.	**(Non) c'è un problema.**	(nohn) cheh oon proh-**blay**-mah
It's good.	**Va bene.**	vah **behn**-ay
You are very kind.	**Lei è molto gentile.**	**leh**ee eh **mohl**-toh jehn-**tee**-lay
Goodbye!	**Arrivederci!**	ah-ree-vay-**dehr**-chee

Where?

Where is...?	**Dov'è...?**	doh-**veh**
...a hotel	**...un hotel**	oon oh-**tehl**
...a youth hostel	**...un ostello della gioventù**	oon oh-**stehl**-loh **dehl**-lah joh-vehn-**too**
...a restaurant	**...un ristorante**	oon ree-stoh-**rahn**-tay
...a supermarket	**...un supermercato**	oon soo-pehr-mehr-**kah**-toh
...a pharmacy	**...una farmacia**	**oo**-nah far-mah-**chee**-ah
...a bank	**...una banca**	**oo**-nah **bahn**-kah
...the train station	**...la stazione**	lah staht-see**oh**-nay

...tourist information	...ufficio informazioni	oo-**fee**-choh een-for-maht-**see**oh-nee
...the toilet	...la toilette	lah twah-**leht**-tay
men	uomini, signori	**woh**-mee-nee, seen-**yoh**-ree
women	donne, signore	**don**-nay, seen-**yoh**-ray

How much?

How much is it?	Quanto costa?	**kwahn**-toh **kos**-tah
Write it?	Me lo scrive?	may loh **skree**-vay
Cheap(er).	(Più) economico.	(pew) ay-koh-**noh**-mee-koh
Cheapest.	Il più economico.	eel pew ay-koh-**noh**-mee-koh
Is it free?	È gratis?	eh **grah**-tees
Is it included?	È incluso?	eh een-**kloo**-zoh
Do you have...?	Ha...?	ah
Where can I buy...?	Dove posso comprare...?	**doh**-vay **pos**-soh kohm-**prah**-ray
I would like...	Vorrei....	vor-**rehee**
We would like...	Vorremo...	vor-**ray**-moh
.this.	...questo.	**kweh**-stoh
...just a little.	...un pochino.	oon poh-**kee**-noh
...more.	...di più.	dee pew
...a ticket.	...un biglietto.	oon beel-**yay**-toh
...a room.	...una camera.	**oo**-nah **kah**-may-rah
...the bill.	...il conto.	eel **kohn**-toh

How many?

one	uno	**oo**-noh
two	due	**doo**-ay
three	tre	tray
four	quattro	**kwah**-troh
five	cinque	**cheeng**-kway
six	sei	**sehee**
seven	sette	**seht**-ta
eight	otto	**ot**-toh

nine	**nove**	**nov**-ay
ten	**dieci**	deeay-chee
hundred	**cento**	**chehn**-toh
thousand	**mille**	**mee**-lay

When?

At what time?	**A che ora?**	ah kay **oh**-rah
Just a moment.	**Un momento.**	oon moh-**mayn**-toh
Now.	**Adesso.**	ah-**dehs**-soh
soon / later	**presto / tardi**	**prehs**-toh / **tar**-dee
today / tomorrow	**oggi / domani**	**oh**-jee / doh-**mah**-nee

Be creative! You can combine these survival phrases to say: "Two, please," or "No, thank you," or "I'd like a cheap hotel," or "Cheaper, please?" Please is a magic word in any language. If you want something and you don't know the word for it, just point and say *"Per favore"* (Please). If you know the word for what you want, such as the bill, simply say, *"Il conto, per favore"* (The bill, please).

Struggling with Italian:

Do you speak English?	**Parla inglese?**	**par**-lah een-**glay**-zay
Even a teeny	**Nemmeno un**	nehm-**may**-noh oon
weeny bit?	**pochino?**	poh-**kee**-noh
Please speak English.	**Parli inglese, per favore.**	**par**-lee een-**glay**-zay pehr fah-**voh**-ray
You speak English well.	**Lei parla bene l'inglese.**	lehee **par**-lah **behn**-ay leen-**glay**-zay
I don't speak Italian.	**Non parlo l'italiano.**	nohn **par**-loh lee-tah-leeah-noh
I speak a little Italian.	**Parlo un po' d'italiano.**	**par**-loh oon poh dee-tah-**leeah**-noh

What is this in Italian?	**Come si dice questo in italiano?**	**koh**-may see **dee**-chay **kweh**-stoh een ee-tah-**leeah**-noh
Repeat?	**Ripeta?**	ree-**pay**-tah
Speak slowly.	**Parli lentamente.**	**par**-lee layn-tah-**mayn**-tay
Slower.	**Più lentamente.**	pew layn-tah-**mayn**-tay
I understand.	**Capito.**	kah-**pee**-toh
I don't understand.	**Non capito.**	nohn kah-**pee**-toh
Do you understand?	**Capisce?**	kah-**pee**-shay
What does this mean?	**Cosa significa?**	**koh**-zah seen-**yee**-fee-kah
Write it?	**Me lo scrive?**	may loh **skree**-vay
Does someone there speak English?	**Qualcuno parla inglese?**	kwahl-**koo**-noh **par**-lah een-**glay**-zay
Who speaks English?	**Chi parla l'inglese?**	kee **par**-lah leen-**glay**-zay

Common questions:

How much?	**Quanto?**	**kwahn**-toh
How many?	**Quanti?**	**kwahn**-tee
How long...?	**Quanto tempo...?**	**kwahn**-toh **tehm**-poh
How long is the trip?	**Quanto dura il viaggio?**	**kwahn**-toh **doo**-rah eel veeah-joh
How many minutes?	**Quanti minuti?**	**kwahn**-tee mee-**noo**-tee
How many hours?	**Quante ore?**	**kwahn**-tay oh-ray
How far?	**Quanto dista?**	**kwahn**-toh **dee**-stah
How?	**Come?**	**koh**-may
Is it possible?	**È possibile?**	eh poh-**see**-bee-lay
Is it necessary?	**È necessario?**	eh nay-say-**sah**-reeoh
Can you help me?	**Può aiutarmi?**	pwoh ah-yoo-**tar**-mee
What? (didn't hear)	**Che cosa?**	kay **koh**-zah
What is that?	**Che cos'è quello?**	kay koh-**zeh kway**-loh
What is better?	**Quale è meglio?**	**kwah**-lay eh **mehl**-yoh
What's going on?	**Cosa succede?**	**koh**-zah soo-**chay**-day
When?	**Quando?**	**kwahn**-doh
What time is it?	**Che ora è?**	kay **oh**-rah eh
At what time?	**A che ora?**	ah kay **oh**-rah

On time?	**Puntuale?**	poon-tooah-lay
Late?	**In ritardo?**	een ree-**tar**-doh
When does this...?	**A che ora...?**	ah kay **oh**-rah
...open	**...aprite**	ah-**pree**-tay
...close	**...chiudete**	keeoo-**day**-tay
Do you have...?	**Ha...?**	ah
Can I / Can we...?	**Posso / Possiamo...?**	**pos**-soh / pos-seeah-moh
...have one	**...averne uno**	ah-**vehr**-nay oo-noh
...go free	**...andare senza pagare**	ahn-**dah**-ray **sehn**-sah pah-**gah**-ray
Where is...?	**Dov'è...?**	doh-**veh**
Where are...?	**Dove sono...?**	**doh**-vay **soh**-noh
Where can I find...?	**Dove posso trovare...?**	**doh**-vay **pos**-soh troh-**vah**-ray
Who?	**Chi?**	kee
Why?	**Perchè?**	pehr-**keh**
Why not?	**Perchè no?**	pehr-**keh** noh
Yes or no?	**Si o no?**	see oh noh

To prompt a simple answer, ask, *"Si o no?"* (Yes or no?). To turn a word or sentence into a question, ask it in a questioning tone. *"Va bene"* (It's good) becomes *"Va bene?"* (Is it good?). An easy way to say, "Where is the toilet?" is to ask, *"Toilette?"*

Yin and yang:

cheap / expensive	**economico / caro**	ay-koh-**noh**-mee-koh /**kah**-roh
big / small	**grande / piccolo**	**grahn**-day / **pee**-koh-loh
hot / cold	**caldo / freddo**	**kahl**-doh / **fray**-doh
open / closed	**aperto / chiuso**	ah-**pehr**-toh / keeoo-zoh
entrance / exit	**entrata / uscita**	ehn-**trah**-tah / oo-**shee**-tah
push / pull	**spingere / tirare**	speen-**gay**-ray / tee-**rah**-ray
arrive / depart	**arrivare / partire**	ah-ree-**vah**-ray / par-**tee**-ray
early / late	**presto / tardi**	**prehs**-toh / **tar**-dee

soon / later	**presto / più tardi**	prehs-toh / pew **tar**-dee
fast / slow	**veloce / lento**	vay-**loh**-chay / **lehn**-toh
here / there	**qui / lì**	kwee / lee
near / far	**vicino / lontano**	vee-**chee**-noh / lohn-**tah**-noh
indoors / outdoors	**dentro / fuori**	**dehn**-troh / foo-**oh**-ree
good / bad	**buono / cattivo**	**bwoh**-noh / kah-**tee**-voh
best / worst	**il migliore / il peggiore**	eel meel-**yoh**-ray / eel pay-**joh**-ray
a little / lots	**poco / tanto**	**poh**-koh / **tahn**-toh
more / less	**più / meno**	pew / **may**-noh
mine / yours	**mio / suo**	**mee**-oh / **soo**-oh
everybody / nobody	**tutti / nessuno**	**too**-tee / nehs-**soo**-noh
easy / difficult	**facile / difficile**	**fah**-chee-lay / dee-**fee**-chee-lay
left / right	**sinistra / destra**	see-**nee**-strah / **dehs**-trah
up / down	**su / giú**	soo / joo
above / below	**sopra / sotto**	**soh**-prah / **soh**-toh
young / old	**giovane / anziano**	joh-**vah**-nay / ahnt-see-**ah**-noh
new / old	**nuovo / vecchio**	**nwoh**-voh / **vehk**-eeoh
heavy / light	**pesante / leggero**	pay-**zahn**-tay / lay-**jay**-roh
light / dark	**chiaro / scuro**	keeah-roh / **skoo**-roh
happy / sad	**felice / triste**	fee-**lee**-chay / **tree**-stay
beautiful / ugly	**bello[a] / brutto[a]**	**behl**-loh / **broo**-toh
nice / mean	**carino[a] / cattivo[a]**	kah-**ree**-noh / kah-**tee**-voh
intelligent / stupid	**intelligente / stupido[a]**	een-tehl-ee-**jayn**-tay / **stoo**-pee-doh
vacant / occupied	**libero / occupato**	**lee**-bay-roh / oh-koo-**pah**-toh
with / without	**con / senza**	kohn / **sehn**-sah

Big little words:

I	**Io**	**ee**oh
you (formal)	**Lei**	**leh**ee
you (informal)	**tu**	too
we	**noi**	**noh**ee

he	**lui**	lwee
she	**lei**	lehee
they	**loro**	loh-roh
and	**e**	ay
at	**a**	ah
because	**perchè**	pehr-**keh**
but	**ma**	mah
by (via)	**in**	een
for	**per**	pehr
from	**da**	dah
here	**qui**	kwee
if	**se**	say
in	**in**	een
not	**non**	nohn
now	**adesso**	ah-**dehs**-soh
only	**solo**	**soh**-loh
or	**o**	oh
this / that	**questo / quello**	**kweh**-stoh / **kweh**-loh
to	**a**	ah
very	**molto**	**mohl**-toh

L'Alphabet:

In case you need to spell your name out loud or participate in a spelling bee...

a	ah	**j**	ee **loon**-goh	**s**	**ehs**-ay
b	bee	**k**	**kahp**-ah	**t**	tee
c	chee	**l**	**ehl**-ay	**u**	oo
d	dee	**m**	**ehm**-ay	**v**	vee
e	ay	**n**	**ehn**-ay	**w**	**dohp**-yah vee
f	**ehf**-ay	**o**	oh	**x**	eeks
g	jee	**p**	pee	**y**	**eep**-see-lohn
h	**ahk**-ah	**q**	koo	**z**	**tseht**-ah
i	ee	**r**	**ehr**-ay		

When spelling out "i" or "e" over the phone, say, *"i, Italia"* or *"e, Empoli"* to make sure you're understood.

Handy Italian expressions:

Prego.	**pray**-goh	You're welcome. / Please. / All right. / Can I help you?
Pronto.	**pron**-toh	Hello. (answering phone) / Ready. (other situations)
Ecco.	**ay**-koh	Here it is.
Dica.	**dee** kah	Tell me.
Senta.	**sayn**-tah	Listen.
Tutto va bene.	**too**-toh vah **behn**-ay	Everything's fine.
È basta.	eh **bah**-stah	That's enough.
È tutto.	eh **too**-toh	That's all.
la dolce vita	lah **dohl**-chay **vee**-tah	the sweet life
il dolce far niente	eel **dohl**-chay far **neeehn**-tay	the sweetness of doing nothing
...issimo[a]	...**ee**-see-moh	very ("bravo" means good, "bravissimo" means very good)

Italian names for places:

Italy	**Italia**	ee-**tahl**-yah
Germany	**Germania**	jehr-**mahn**-yah
Munich	**Monaco di Baviera**	**moh**-nah-koh dee bah-**veeay**-rah
France	**Francia**	**frahn**-chah
Paris	**Parigi**	pah-**ree**-jee
England	**Inghilterra**	een-geel-**tehr**-rah
Netherlands	**Paesi Bassi**	pah-**ay**-zee **bah**-see
Austria	**Austria**	**ow**-streeah
Switzerland	**Svizzera**	**sveet**-say-rah

BASICS

Spain	**Spagna**	**spahn**-yah
Greece	**Grecia**	**gray**-chah
Turkey	**Turchia**	**toor**-keeah
Europe	**Europa**	ay-oo-**roh**-pah
Russia	**Russia**	**roo**-seeah
Africa	**Africa**	**ah**-free-kah
United States	**Stati Uniti**	**stah**-tee oo-**nee**-tee
Canada	**Canada**	kah-nah-**dah**
world	**mondo**	**mohn**-doh

Places in Italy:

Bologna	**Bologna**	boh-**lohn**-yah
Cinque Terre	**Cinque Terre**	**cheeng**-kway **tehr**-ray
Civita	**Civita**	chee-**vee**-tah
Florence	**Firenze**	fee-**rehn**-tsay
Italian Riviera	**Riviera Ligure**	reev-**yehr**-rah lee-**goo**-ray
Lake Como	**Lago di Como**	**lah**-goh dee **koh**-moh
Milan	**Milano**	mee-**lah**-noh
Naples	**Napoli**	**nah**-poh-lee
Orvieto	**Orvieto**	or-**veeay**-toh
Pisa	**Pisa**	**pee**-zah
Rome	**Roma**	**roh**-mah
San Gimignano	**San Gimignano**	sahn jee-meen-**yah**-noh
Sicily	**Sicilia**	see-**chee**-leeah
Siena	**Siena**	see-**ehn**-ah
Sorrento	**Sorrento**	sor-**rehn**-toh
Varenna	**Varenna**	vah-**rehn**-nah
Vatican City	**Città del Vaticano**	cheet-**tah** dayl vah-tee-**kah**-noh
Venice	**Venezia**	vay-**nayt**-seeah
Vernazza	**Vernazza**	vehr-**naht**-tsah

Numbers

0	zero	zay-roh
1	uno	oo-noh
2	due	doo-ay
3	tre	tray
4	quattro	kwah-troh
5	cinque	cheeng-kway
6	sei	sehee
7	sette	seht-tay
8	otto	ot-toh
9	nove	nov-ay
10	dieci	deeay-chee
11	undici	oon-dee-chee
12	dodici	doh-dee-chee
13	tredici	tray-dee-chee
14	quattordici	kwah-tor-dee-chee
15	quindici	kween-dee-chee
16	sedici	say-dee-chee
17	diciassette	dee-chahs-seht-tay
18	diciotto	dee-choh-toh
19	diciannove	dee-chahn-nov-ay
20	venti	vayn-tee
21	ventuno	vayn-too-noh
22	ventidue	vayn-tee-doo-ay
23	ventitrè	vayn-tee-tray
30	trenta	trayn-tah
31	trentuno	trayn-too-noh
40	quaranta	kwah-rahn-tah

41	**quarantuno**	kwah-rahn-**too**-noh
50	**cinquanta**	cheeng-**kwahn**-tah
60	**sessanta**	say-**sahn**-tah
70	**settanta**	say-**tahn**-tah
80	**ottanta**	ot-**tahn**-tah
90	**novanta**	noh-**vahn**-tah
100	**cento**	**chehn**-toh
101	**centouno**	chehn-toh-**oo**-noh
102	**centodue**	chehn-toh-**doo**-ay
200	**duecento**	doo-ay-**chehn**-toh
1000	**mille**	**mee**-lay
2000	**duemila**	doo-ay-**mee**-lah
2001	**duemilauno**	doo-ay-mee-lah-**oo**-noh
10,000	**diecimila**	deeay-chee-**mee**-lah
million	**milione**	mee-leeoh-nay
billion	**miliardo**	meel-**yar**-doh
first	**primo**	**pree**-moh
second	**secondo**	say-**kohn**-doh
third	**terzo**	**tehrt**-soh
half	**mezzo**	**mehd**-zoh
100%	**cento per cento**	**chehn**-toh pehr **chehn**-toh
number one	**numero uno**	**noo**-may-roh **oo**-noh

NUMBERS

Money

| Can you change dollars? | **Può cambiare dollari?** | pwoh kahm-beeah-ray **dol**-lah-ree |
| What is your exchange rate for dollars...? | **Qual'è il cambio del dollari...?** | kwah-**leh** eel **kahm**-beeoh dayl **dol**-lah-ree |

...in traveler's checks	**...per traveler's checks**	pehr "traveler's checks"
What is the commission?	**Quant'è la commissione?**	kwahn-**teh** lah koh-mee-seeoh-nay
Any extra fee?	**C'è un sovrapprezzo?**	cheh oon soh-vrah-**preht**-soh
I would like...	**Vorrei...**	vor-**rehee**
...small bills.	**...banconote di piccolo taglio.**	bahn-koh-**noh**-tay dee **pee**-koh-loh **tahl**-yoh
...large bills.	**...banconote di grosso taglio.**	bahn-koh-**noh**-tay dee **groh**-soh **tahl**-yoh
...coins.	**...monete.**	moh-**nay**-tay
Is this a mistake?	**Questo è un errore?**	**kweh**-stoh eh oon eh-**roh**-ray
I'm rich.	**Sono ricco[a].**	**soh**-noh **ree**-koh
I'm poor.	**Sono povero[a].**	**soh**-noh **poh**-vay-roh
I'm broke.	**Sono al verde.**	**soh**-noh ahl **vehr**-day
euro	**euro**	**yoo**-roh
Where is a cash machine?	**Dov'è un bancomat?**	doh-**veh** oon **bahnk**-oh-maht

Bank fees can be steep—cash machines are your best bet. At a *bancomat* (cash machine), use your *codice segreto* (PIN number) to *ritirare* (withdraw) money from your *conto corrente* (checking account). You can *conferma* (confirm), *annullare* (cancel), or *esatto* (correct).

Key money words:

bank	**banca**	**bahn**-kah
money	**soldi, denaro**	**sohl**-dee, day-**nah**-roh
change money	**cambiare dei soldi**	kahm-beeah-ray **dehee sohl**-dee
exchange	**cambio**	**kahm**-beeoh
buy / sell	**comprare / vendere**	kohm-**prah**-ray / vehn-**day**-ray
commission	**commissione**	koh-mee-seeoh-nay
traveler's check	**traveler's check**	"traveler's check"
check	**assegno**	ah-**cohn**-yoh
credit card	**carta di credito**	**kar**-tah dee **kray**-dee-toh
cash advance	**prelievo**	pray-leeay-voh
cash machine	**bancomat**	**bahnk**-oh-maht
cashier	**cassiere**	kah-seeay-ray
cash	**contante**	kohn-**tahn**-tay
bills	**banconote**	bahn-koh-**noh**-tay
coins	**monete**	moh-**nay**-tay
receipt	**ricevuta**	ree-chay-**voo**-tah

MONEY

Time

What time is it?	Che ore sono?	kay oh-ray **soh**-noh
It's...	Sono...	**soh**-noh
...8:00.	...le otto.	lay ot-toh
...16:00.	...le sedici.	lay **say**-dee-chee
...4:00 in the afternoon.	...le quattro del pomeriggio.	lay **kwah**-troh dayl poh-may-**ree**-joh
...10:30 (in the evening).	...le dieci e mezza (di sera).	lay deeay-chee ay **mehd**-tsah (dee **say**-rah)
...a quarter past nine.	...le nove e un quarto.	lay **nov**-ay ay oon **kwar**-toh
...a quarter to eleven.	...le undici meno un quarto.	lay **oon**-dee-chee **may**-noh oon **kwar**-toh
It's...	È...	eh
...noon.	...mezzogiorno.	mehd-zoh-**jor**-noh
...midnight.	...mezzanotte.	mehd-zah-**not**-tay
...sunrise / sunset.	...alba / tramonto.	**ahl**-bah / trah-**mohn**-toh
...early / late.	...presto / tardi.	**prehs**-toh / **tar**-dee
...on time.	...puntuale.	poon-tooah-lay

In Italy, the 24-hour clock (or military time) is used by hotels, for opening/closing hours of stores, and for train, bus, and ferry schedules. Friends use the same "clock" we do. You'd meet a friend at 3:00 in the afternoon (*3:00 del pomeriggio*) to catch a train that leaves at 15:15. In Italy, the *pomeriggio* (afternoon) turns to *sera* (evening) generally about 5:00 p.m. (5:30 p.m. is *cinque e mezza di sera*).

Timely words:

minute	**minuto**	mee-**noo**-toh
hour	**ora**	**oh**-rah
morning	**mattina**	mah-**tee**-nah
afternoon	**pomeriggio**	poh-may-**ree**-joh
evening	**sera**	**say**-rah
night	**notte**	**not**-tay
day	**giorno**	**jor**-noh
today	**oggi**	**oh**-jee
yesterday	**ieri**	**yay**-ree
tomorrow	**domani**	doh-**mah**-nee
tomorrow morning	**domani mattina**	doh-**mah**-nee mah-**tee**-nah
day after tomorrow	**dopodomani**	doh-poh-doh-**mah**-nee
anytime	**a qualsiasi ora**	ah kwahl-see**ah**-zee **oh**-rah
immediately	**immediatamente**	ee-may-deeah-tah-**mayn**-tay
in one hour	**tra un'ora**	trah oon-**oh**-rah
every hour	**ogni ora**	**ohn**-yee **oh**-rah
every day	**ogni giorno**	**ohn**-yee **jor**-noh
last	**passato**	pah-**sah**-toh
this	**questo**	**kweh**-stoh
next	**prossimo**	**pros**-see-moh
May 15	**il quindici di maggio**	eel **kween**-dee-chee dee **mah**-joh
high / low season	**alta / bassa stagione**	**ahl**-tah / **bah**-sah stah-jee**oh**-nee
in the future	**in futuro**	een foo-**too**-roh
in the past	**nel passato**	nehl pah-**sah**-toh

week	**settimana**	say-tee-**mah**-nah
Monday	**lunedì**	loo-nay-**dee**
Tuesday	**martedì**	mar-tay-**dee**
Wednesday	**mercoledì**	mehr-koh-lay-**dee**
Thursday	**giovedì**	joh-vay-**dee**
Friday	**venerdì**	vay-nehr-**dee**
Saturday	**sabato**	**sah**-bah-toh
Sunday	**domenica**	doh-**may**-nee-kah
month	**mese**	**may**-zay
January	**gennaio**	jay-**nah**-yoh
February	**febbraio**	fay-**brah**-yoh
March	**marzo**	**mart**-soh
April	**aprile**	ah-**pree**-lay
May	**maggio**	**mah**-joh
June	**giugno**	**joon**-yoh
July	**luglio**	**lool**-yoh
August	**agosto**	ah-**goh**-stoh
September	**settembre**	say-**tehm**-bray
October	**ottobre**	oh-**toh**-bray
November	**novembre**	noh-**vehm**-bray
December	**dicembre**	dee-**chehm**-bray
year	**anno**	**ahn**-noh
spring	**primavera**	pree-mah-**vay**-rah
summer	**estate**	ay-**stah**-tay
fall	**autunno**	ow-**too**-noh
winter	**inverno**	een-**vehr**-noh

Italian holidays and happy days:

holiday	**festa**	**fehs**-tah
national holiday	**festa nazionale**	**fehs**-tah naht-seeoh-**nah**-lay
religious holiday	**festa religiosa**	**fehs**-tah ray-lee-**joh**-zah
Is today / tomorrow a holiday?	**Oggi / Domani è festa?**	**oh**-jee / doh-**mah**-nee eh **fehs**-tah
What is the holiday?	**Che festa è?**	kay **fehs**-tah eh
Easter	**Pasqua**	**pahs**-kwah
Merry Christmas!	**Buon Natale!**	bwohn nah-**tah**-lay
Happy new year!	**Felice anno nuovo!**	fay-**lee**-chay **ahn**-noh **noooh**-voh
Happy birthday!	**Buon compleanno!**	bwohn kohm-play-**ahn**-noh

TIME

Italians celebrate birthdays with the same "Happy birthday" tune that we use. The Italian words mean "Best wishes to you": *Tanti auguri a te, tanti auguri a te, tanti auguri, caro[a] ___, tanti auguri a te!"*

Holidays which strike during tourist season are April 25th (Liberation Day), May 1st (Labor Day), June 24th (*San Giovanni*, northern Italy), August 15th (*Ferragosto*, or Ascension of Mary), and November 1st (All Saints Day). In Italy, every saint gets a holiday—these are sprinkled throughout the year and celebrated in local communities with flair.

Transportation

- Trains 22
- Buses and subways 29
- Taxis 31
- Rental wheels 33
- Driving 34
- Finding your way 37

Trains:

Is this the line for...?	È questa la fila per...?	eh kweh-stah lah fee-lah pehr
...tickets	...biglietti	beel-yay-tee
...reservations	...prenotazioni	pray-noh-taht-seeoh-nee
How much is the fare to...?	Quant'è la tariffa per...?	kwahn-teh lah tah-ree-fah pehr
A ticket to ___.	Un biglietto per ___.	oon beel-yay-toh pehr
When is the next train?	Quando è il prossimo treno?	kwahn-doh eh eel pros-see-moh tray-noh
I'd like to leave...	Vorrei partire...	vor-rehee par-tee-ray
I'd like to arrive...	Vorrei arrivare...	vor-rehee ah-ree-vah-ray
...by ___.	...per le ___.	pehr lay
...in the morning.	...la mattina.	lah mah-tee-nah
...in the afternoon.	...il pomeriggio.	eel poh-may-ree-joh
...in the evening.	...la sera.	lah say-rah
Is there a...?	C'è un...?	cheh oon
..earlier train	...treno prima	tray-noh pree-mah

...later train	...treno più tardi	**tray**-noh pew **tar**-dee
...overnight train	...treno notturno	**tray**-noh noh-**toor**-noh
...supplement	...supplemento	soo-play-**mehn**-toh
Does my railpass cover the supplement?	Il mio railpass include il supplemento?	eel **mee**-oh **rayl**-pahs een-**kloo**-day eel soo-play-**mehn**-toh
Is there a discount for...?	Fate sconti per...?	**fah**-tay **skohn**-tee pehr
...youths / seniors	...giovani / anziani	joh-**vah**-nee / ahnt-seeah-nee
Is a reservation required?	Ci vuole la prenotazione?	chee **vwoh**-lay lah pray-noh-taht-seeoh-nay
I'd like to reserve...	Vorrei prenotare...	vor-**rehee** pray-noh-**tah**-ray
...a seat.	...un posto.	oon **poh**-stoh
...a berth.	...una cuccetta.	**oo**-nah koo-**chay**-tah
...a sleeper.	...un posto in vagone letto.	oon **poh**-stoh een vah-**goh**-nay **leht**-toh
Where does (the train) leave from?	Da dove parte?	dah **doh**-vay **par**-tay
What track?	Quale binario?	**kwah**-lay bee-**nah**-reeoh
On time?	È puntuale?	eh poon-tooah-lay
Late?	In ritardo?	een ree-**tar**-doh
When will it arrive?	Quando arriva?	**kwahn**-doh ah-**ree**-vah
Is it direct?	È diretto?	eh dee-**reht**-toh
Must I transfer?	Devo cambiare?	**day**-voh kahm-beeah-ray
When? / Where?	Quando? / Dove?	**kwahn**-doh / **doh**-vay
Which train to...?	Quale treno per....?	**kwah**-lay **tray**-noh pehr
Which train car to...?	Quale vagone per....?	**kwah**-lay vah-**goh**-nay pehr
Where is first class?	Dov'è la prima classe?	doh-**veh** lah **pree**-mah **klah**-say

...front / middle / back	**in testa / in centro / in coda**	een **tehs**-tah / een **chehn**-troh / een **koh**-dah
Is this (seat) free?	**È libero?**	eh **lee**-bay-roh
It's my seat.	**È il mio posto.**	eh eel **mee**-oh **poh**-stoh
Save my place?	**Mi tenga il posto?**	mee **tayn**-gah eel **poh**-stoh
Where are you going?	**Dove va?**	**doh**-vay vah
I'm going to...	**Vado a...**	**vah**-doh ah
Tell me when to get off?	**Mi dica quando devo scendere?**	mee **dee**-kah **kwahn**-doh **day**-voh **shehn**-day-ray
Is there a train to the airport?	**C'è un treno che va all'aereoporto?**	cheh oon **tray**-noh kay vah ahl-ay-ray-oh-**por**-toh
Is there a train from the airport to...?	**C'è un treno che viene dall'aereoporto a...?**	cheh oon **tray**-noh kay vee-**ehn**-ay dahl-ay-ray-oh-**por**-toh ah

Ticket talk:

ticket window	**Biglietteria**	beel-yeht-ay-**ree**-ah
reservations window	**Prenotazioni**	pray-noh-taht-see**oh**-nay
national	**nazionali**	naht-seeoh-**nah**-lee
international	**internazionali**	een-tehr-naht-seeoh-**nah**-lee
ticket	**biglietto**	beel-**yay**-toh
one way	**andata**	ahn-**dah**-tah
roundtrip	**andata e ritorno**	ahn-**dah**-tah ay ree-**tor**-noh
first class	**prima classe**	**pree**-mah **klah**-say
second class	**seconda classe**	say-**kohn**-dah **klah**-say
non-smoking	**non fumare**	nohn foo-**mah**-ray
reduced fare	**tariffa ridotta**	tah-**ree**-fah ree-**doh**-tah
validate	**obliterare**	oh-blee-tay-**rah**-ray
schedule	**orario**	oh-**rah**-reeoh
departure	**partenza**	par-**tehnt**-sah

direct	**diretto**	dee-**reht**-toh
transfer (verb)	**cambiare**	kahm-beeah-ray
connection	**coincidenza**	koh-een-chee-**dehnt**-sah
with supplement	**con supplemento**	kohn soo-play-**mehn**-toh
reservation	**prenotazione**	pray-noh-taht-seeoh-nay
seat	**posto**	**poh**-stoh
seat by...	**posto vicino...**	**poh**-stoh vee-**chee**-noh
...the window	**...al finestrino**	ahl fee-nay-**stree**-noh
...the aisle	**...al corridoio**	ahl kor-ree-**doh**-yoh
berth...	**cuccetta...**	koo-**chay**-tah
...upper	**...di sopra**	dee **soh**-prah
...middle	**...in mezzo**	een **mehd**-zoh
...lower	**...di sotto**	dee **soh**-toh
refund	**rimborso**	reem-**bor**-soh

You must *obliterare* (validate) your train ticket prior to boarding the train. Look for the yellow machines on the platform and insert your ticket—watch others and imitate.

At the train station:

Italian State Railways	**Ferrovie dello Stato (FS)**	fay-**roh**-veeay **dehl**-loh **stah**-toh
train station	**stazione**	staht-seeoh-nay
train information	**informazioni sui treni**	een-for-maht-seeoh-nee sooee **tray**-nee
train	**treno**	**tray**-noh
fast train	**inter-city (IC, EC)**	"inter-city"
fastest train	**Eurostar (ES)**	**yoo**-roh-star
arrival	**arrivo**	ah-**ree**-voh

departure	**partenza**	par-**tehnt**-sah
delay	**ritardo**	ree-**tar**-doh
toilet	**toilette**	twah-**leht**-tay
waiting room	**sala di attesa,**	**sah**-lah dee ah-**tay**-zah,
	sala d'aspetto	**sah**-lah dah-**spay**-toh
lockers	**armadietti**	ar-mah-deeay-tee
baggage check room	**deposito bagagli,**	day-**poh**-zee-toh bah-**gahl**-
	consegna	yee, kohn-**sayn**-yah
lost and found office	**ufficio oggetti**	oo-**fee**-choh oh-**jeht**-tee
	smarriti	smah-**ree**-tee
tourist information	**informazioni per**	een-for-maht-seeoh-nee pehr
	turisti	too-**ree**-stee
to the trains	**ai treni**	ahee **tray**-nee
track or platform	**binario**	bee-**nah**-reeoh
train car	**vagone**	vah-**goh**-nay
dining car	**carrozza ristorante**	kar-**rot**-sah ree-stoh-**rahn**-tay
sleeper car	**carrozza letto**	kar-**rot**-sah **leht**-toh
conductor	**controllore**	kohn-troh-**loh**-ray

Strikes:

Is there a strike?	**C'è lo sciopero?**	cheh loh **shoh**-peh-roh
Only for today?	**È solo per oggi?**	eh **soh**-loh pehr **oh**-jee
Tomorrow, too?	**Anche domani?**	**ahn**-kay doh-**mah**-nee
Are there some trains today?	**Ci sono qualcuni treni oggi?**	chee **soh**-noh kwahl-**koo**-nee **tray**-nee **oh**-jee
I'm going to...	**Vado a...**	**vah**-doh ah

Major rail lines in Italy

TRANSPORTATION

KEY: — RAIL --- BUS .... SHIP
NOT TO SCALE ● OVERNIGHT STOPS (ON 22 DAYS ROUTE)

—DCH—

In Italy, train strikes (*scioperi*) are not unusual. They often last a day and a few trains still run, particularly the long-distance routes.

Reading train schedules:

a	to
arrivi	arrivals
arrivo	arrival (also abbreviated "a")
binario	track
da	from
destinazione	destination
domenica	Sunday
eccetto	except
feriali	weekdays including Saturday
ferma a tutte le stazioni	stops at all the stations
festivi	Sundays and holidays
fino	until
giorni	days
giornaliero	daily
in ritardo	late
non ferma a...	doesn't stop in...
ogni	every
partenza	departure (also abbreviated "p")
partenze	departures
per	for
sabato	Saturday
si effettua anche...	it also runs...
solo	only
tutti i giorni	daily
vacanza	holiday
1-5	Monday-Friday
6, 7	Saturday, Sunday

Italian schedules use the 24-hour clock. It's like American time until noon. After that, subtract twelve and add p.m. So 13:00 is 1 p.m., 20:00 is 8 p.m., and 24:00 is midnight. If your train is scheduled to depart at 00:01, it'll leave one minute after midnight.

Italian train stations have wonderful (and fun) new schedule computers. Once you've mastered these (start by punching the "English" button), you'll save lots of time figuring out the right train connections. Italian trains come in five types: the slow milk-run *locale*, the slightly faster *diretto*, the *espresso* which stops only at big stations, the speedy *rapido* (also called *IC* or *EC*), and finally, the *Eurostar*, Italy's bullet train. If you have a train pass, you won't have to pay the supplement for Italy's fast trains, but you (and everyone else) will need to make a reservation for the *Eurostar*.

Buses and subways:

How do I get to...?	**Come si va a...?**	**koh**-may see vah ah
Which bus to...?	**Quale autobus per....?**	**kwah**-lay **ow**-toh-boos pehr
Does it stop at...?	**Si ferma a...?**	see **fehr**-mah ah
Which metro stop for...?	**A quale stazione scendo per...?**	ah **kway**-lay staht-see**oh**-nay **shehn**-doh pehr
Which direction for...?	**Da che parte è...?**	dah kay **par**-tay eh
Must I transfer?	**Devo cambiare?**	**day**-voh kahm-bee**ah**-ray
How much is a ticket?	**Quanto costa un biglietto?**	**kwahn**-toh **kos**-tah oon beel-**yay**-toh

TRANSPORTATION

Where can I buy a ticket?	**Dove posso comprare un biglietto?**	doh-vay pos-soh kohm-prah-ray oon beel-yay-toh
Is there a one-day pass?	**C'è un biglietto giornaliero?**	cheh oon beel-yay-toh jor-nahl-yay-roh
When is the...?	**Quando parte...?**	kwahn-doh par-tay
...first / next / last	**...il primo / il prossimo / l'ultimo**	eel pree-moh / eel pros-see-moh / lool-tee-moh
...bus / subway	**...l'autobus / la metropolitana**	low-toh-boos / lah may-troh-poh-lee-tah-nah
What's the frequency per hour / day?	**Quante volte passa all'ora / al giorno?**	kwahn-tay vohl-tay pah-sah ahl-loh-rah / ahl jor-noh
I'm going to...	**Vado a...**	vah-doh ah
Tell me when to get off?	**Mi dica quando devo scendere?**	mee dee-kah kwahn-doh day-voh shehn-day-ray
Is there a bus to the airport?	**C'è un autobus che va all'aereoporto?**	cheh oon ow-toh-boos kay vah ahl-ay-ray-oh-por-toh
Is there a bus from the airport to...?	**C'è un autobus che viene dall'aereoporto a...?**	cheh oon ow-toh-boos kay vee-ehn-ay dahl-ay-ray-oh-por-toh ah

Key bus and subway words:

ticket	**biglietto**	beel-yay-toh
city bus	**autobus**	ow-toh-boos
long-distance bus	**pullman, corriera**	pool-mahn, koh-ree-ehr-ah
bus stop	**fermata**	fehr-mah-tah
bus station	**stazione degli autobus**	staht-seeoh-nay dayl-yee ow-toh-boos
subway	**metropolitana**	may-troh-poh-lee-tah-nah
entrance	**entrata**	ayn-trah-tah

stop	**fermata**	fehr-**mah**-tah
exit	**uscita**	oo-**shee**-tah
direct	**diretto**	dee-**reht**-toh
connection	**coincidenza**	koh-een-chee-**dehnt**-sah
map	**cartina**	kar-**tee**-nah
pickpocket	**borsaiolo**	bor-sah-**yoh**-loh

Venice has boats instead of buses. Zip around on *traghetti* (gondola ferries) and *vaporetti* (motorized ferries).

Taxis:

Taxi!	**Taxi!**	**tahk**-see
Can you call a taxi?	**Può chiamare un taxi?**	pwoh kee-ah-**mah**-ray oon **tahk**-see
Where is a taxi stand?	**Dov'è una fermata dei taxi?**	doh-**veh** oo-nah fehr-**mah**-tah dehee **tahk**-see
Are you free?	**È libero?**	eh **lee**-bay-roh
Occupied.	**Occupato.**	oh-koo-**pah**-toh
How much is it...?	**Quanto costa fino...?**	**kwahn**-toh **kos**-tah **fee**-noh
...to the airport	**...all'aereoporto**	ah-lah-ay-ray-oh-**por**-toh
...to the train station	**...alla stazione ferroviaria**	**ah**-lah staht-see**oh**-nay fay-roh-vee-**ah**-reeah
...to this address	**...a questo indirizzo**	ah **kweh**-stoh een-dee-**reet**-soh
Too much.	**Troppo.**	**trop**-poh
This is all I have.	**Questo è tutto quello che ho.**	**kweh**-stoh eh **too**-toh **kwehl**-loh kay oh
Can you take ___ people?	**Può portar ___ persone?**	pwoh **por**-tar ___ pehr-**soh**-nay

English	Italian	Pronunciation
Any extra fee?	C'è un sovrapprezzo?	cheh oon soh-vrah-**preht**-soh
The meter, please.	Il tassametro, per favore.	eel tah-sah-**may**-troh pehr fah-**voh**-ray
Where is the meter?	Dov'è il tassametro?	doh-**veh** eel tah-sah-**may**-troh
The most direct route.	Il percorso più breve.	eel pehr-**kor**-soh pew bray-vay
I'm in a hurry.	Sono di fretta.	soh-noh dee fray-tah
Slow down.	Rallenti.	rah-**lehn**-tee
If you don't slow down, I'll throw up.	Se non rallenta, vomito.	say nohn rah-**lehn**-tah, voh-mee-toh
Stop here.	Si fermi qui.	see **fehr**-mee kwee
Can you wait?	Può aspettare?	pwoh ah-spay-**tah**-ray
I'll never forget this ride.	Non dimenticherò mai questo viaggio.	nohn dee-mayn-tee-kay-**roh** mahee kweh-stoh veeah-joh
Where did you learn to drive?	Ma dove ha imparato a guidare?	mah doh-vay ah eem-pah-**rah**-toh ah gwee-**dah**-ray
I'll only pay what's on the meter.	Pago solo la cifra sul tassametro.	pah-goh soh-loh lah chee-frah sool tah-sah-**may**-troh
My change, please.	Il resto, per favore.	eel rehs-toh pehr fah-**voh**-ray
Keep the change.	Tenga il resto.	tayn-gah eel rehs-toh

Tipping is not necessary, but if you've had a particularly helpful driver, round up to the nearest euro (and add another euro if you wish). Cab fares are reasonable and most drivers are honest. Expect a charge for luggage. Three or more tourists are usually better off hailing a cab than messing with city buses in Italy. If cabs won't stop for you, your luck may improve at a nearby *fermata dei taxi* (taxi stand).

Rental wheels:

I'd like to rent...	**Vorrei noleggiare...**	vor-**reh**ee noh-leh-**jah**-ree
...a car.	**...una macchina.**	**oo**-nah **mah**-kee-nah
...a station wagon.	**...una station wagon.**	**oo**-nah **staht**-see-ohn **wah**-gohn
...a van.	**...un monovolume.**	oon moh-noh-voh-**loo**-may
...a motorcycle.	**...una motocicletta.**	**oo**-nah moh-toh-chee-**klay**-tah
...a motor scooter.	**...un motorino.**	oon moh-toh-**ree**-noh
...a bicycle.	**...una bicicletta.**	**oo**-nah bee-chee-**klay**-tah
How much...?	**Quanto...?**	**kwahn**-toh
...per hour	**...all'ora**	ah-**loh**-rah
...per day	**...al giorno**	ahl **jor**-noh
...per week	**...alla settimana**	**ah**-lah say-tee-**mah**-nah
Unlimited mileage?	**Chilometraggio illimitato?**	kee-loh-may-**trah**-joh eel-lee-mee-**tah**-toh
I brake for bakeries.	**Mi fermo ad ogni pasticceria.**	mee **fehr**-moh ahd **ohn**-yee pah-stee-chay-**ree**-ah
Is there...?	**C'è...?**	cheh
...a helmet	**...un casco**	oon **kah**-skoh
...a discount	**...uno sconto**	**oo**-noh **skohn**-toh
...a deposit	**...una caparra**	**oo**-nah kah-**pah**-rah
...insurance	**...l'assicurazione**	lah-see-koo-raht-see**oh**-nay
When do I bring it back?	**Quando lo riporto indietro?**	**kwahn**-doh loh ree-**por**-toh een-dee**ay**-troh

Driving:

gas station	**benzinaio**	baynd-zee-**nah**-yoh
The nearest gas station?	**Il benzinaio più vicino?**	eel baynd-zee-**nah**-yoh pew vee-**chee**-noh
Self-service?	**Self-service?**	"self service"
Fill the tank.	**Il pieno.**	eel peeay-noh
I need...	**Ho bisogno di...**	oh bee-**zohn**-yoh dee
...gas.	**...benzina.**	baynd-**zee**-nah
...unleaded.	**...benzina verde.**	baynd-**zee**-nah **vehr**-day
...regular.	**...normale.**	nor-**mah**-lay
...super.	**...super.**	**soo**-pehr
...diesel.	**...gasolio.**	gah-**zoh**-leeoh
Check...	**Controlli...**	kohn-**troh**-lee
...the oil.	**...l'olio.**	**loh**-leeoh
...the tires.	**...le gomme.**	lay **goh**-may
...the radiator.	**...il radiatore.**	eel rah-deeah-**toh**-ray
...the battery.	**...la batteria.**	lah bah-tay-**ree**-ah
...the fuses.	**...i fusibili.**	ee foo-**zee**-bee-lee
...the sparkplugs.	**...le candele.**	lay kahn-**day**-lay
...the headlights.	**...gli anabbaglianti.**	lyee ah-nah-bahl-yee**ahn**-tee
...the tail lights.	**...i luci posteriori.**	ee **loo**-chee pos-tay-ree**oh**-ree
...the directional signal.	**...la freccia.**	lah **freh**-chah
...the car mirror.	**...il specchietto della macchina.**	eel speh-**cheht**-toh **dehl**-lah **mah**-kee-nah
...the fanbelt.	**...la cinghia del ventilatore.**	lah **cheen**-geeah dayl vehn-tee-lah-**toh**-ray
...the brakes.	**...i freni.**	ee **fray**-nee

...my pulse.	...il mio battito cardiaco.	eel mee-oh bah-tee-toh kar-deeah-koh

Filling up the tank in Italy is just like at home, except the pump says euros and liters rather than dollars and gallons. The freeway rest stops and city *automat* gas pumps are the only places that sell gas during the afternoon siesta hours. Gas is always more expensive on the super highways. Italy's famous coupons for cheaper gas (available only to tourists at the border crossings) are not worth the complexity they add to your travels.

Car trouble:

accident	incidente	een-chee-dehn-tay
breakdown	guasto	gooah-stoh
funny noise	rumore strano	roo-moh-ray strah-noh
electrical problem	problema elettrico	proh-blay-mah ay-leht-ree-koh
flat tire	gomma a terra	goh-mah ah tay-rah
dead battery	batteria scarica	bah-tay-ree-ah skah-ree-kah
My car won't start.	La mia macchina non parte.	lah mee-ah mah-kee-nah nohn par-tay
This doesn't work.	Non funziona.	nohn foont-seeoh-nah
It's overheating.	Si sta surriscaldando.	see stah soo-ree-skahl-dahn-doh
It's a lemon (a swindle).	È una fregatura.	eh oo-nah fray-gah-too-rah
I need...	Ho bisogno di...	oh bee-zohn-yoh dee
...a tow truck.	...un carro attrezzi.	oon kar-roh ah-trayt-see

...a mechanic.	**...un meccanico.**	oon may-**kah**-nee-koh
...a stiff drink.	**...un whiskey.**	oon "whiskey"

For help with repair, look up "Repair" under Shopping.

Parking:

parking garage	**garage**	gah-**rahj**
Where can I park?	**Dove posso parcheggiare?**	**doh**-vay **pos**-soh par-kay-**jah**-ray
Is parking nearby?	**È vicino il parcheggio?**	eh vee-**chee**-noh eel par-**kay**-joh
Can I park here?	**Posso parcheggiare qui?**	**pos**-soh par-kay-**jah**-ray kwee
How long can I park here?	**Per quanto tempo posso parcheggiare qui?**	pehr **kwahn**-toh **tehm**-poh **pos**-soh par-kay-**jah**-ray kwee
Must I pay to park here?	**È a pagamento questo parcheggio?**	eh ah pah-gah-**mayn**-toh **kweh**-stoh par-**kay**-joh
Is this a safe place to park?	**È sicuro parcheggiare qui?**	eh see-**koo**-roh par-kay-**jah**-ray kwee

Parking in Italian cities is expensive and hazardous. Plan to pay to use a parking garage in big cities. Leave nothing in your car at night. Always ask at your hotel about safe parking. Take parking restrictions seriously to avoid getting fines and having your car towed away (an interesting but costly experience).

Finding your way:

I am going to...	**Vado a...**	**vah**-doh ah
How do I get to...?	**Come si va a...?**	**koh**-may see vah ah
Is there a map?	**C'è una cartina?**	cheh **oo**-nah kar-**tee**-nah
How many minutes...?	**Quanti minuti...?**	**kwahn**-tee mee-**noo**-tee
How many hours...?	**Quante ore...?**	**kwahn**-tay oh-ray
...on foot	**...a piedi**	ah peeay-dee
...by bicycle	**...in bicicletta**	een bee-chee-**klay**-tah
...by car	**...in macchina**	een **mah**-kee-nah
How many kilometers to...?	**Quanti chilometri per...?**	**kwahn**-tee kee-**loh**-may-tree pehr
What is the...	**Qual'è la strada...**	kwah-**leh** lah **strah**-dah...
route to Rome?	**per andare a Roma?**	pehr ahn-**dah**-ray ah **roh**-mah
...best	**...migliore**	meel-**yoh**-ray
...fastest	**...più veloce**	pew vay-**loh**-chay
...most interesting	**...più interessante**	pew een-tay-ray-**sahn**-tay
Point it out?	**Me lo mostri?**	may loh **mohs**-tree
I'm lost.	**Mi sono perso[a].**	mee **soh**-noh **pehr**-soh
Where am I?	**Dove sono?**	**doh**-vay **soh**-noh
Who am I?	**Chi sono?**	kee **soh**-noh
Where is...?	**Dov'è...?**	doh-**veh**
The nearest...?	**Il più vicino...?**	eel pew vee-**chee**-noh
Where is this address?	**Dov'è questo indirizzo?**	doh-**veh kweh**-stoh een-dee-**reet**-soh

In Italy, the shortest distance between any two points is the *autostrada*, though the tolls are not cheap (about a dollar for each ten minutes). There are not as many signs as we are used to, so stay alert or you may miss your exit! Italy's *autostrada* rest stops are among the best in Europe.

Key route-finding words:

map	**cartina**	kar-**tee**-nah
road map	**cartina stradale**	kar-**tee**-nah strah-**dah**-lay
downtown	**centro**	**chehn**-troh
straight ahead	**sempre diritto**	**sehm**-pray dee-**ree**-toh
left / right	**sinistra / destra**	see-**nee**-strah / **dehs**-trah
first / next	**prima / prossima**	**pree**-mah / **pros**-see-mah
intersection	**incrocio**	een-**kroh**-choh
stoplight	**semaforo**	say-mah-**foh**-roh
roundabout	**rotonda**	roh-**ton**-dah
(main) square	**piazza (principale)**	peeaht-sah (preen-chee-**pah**-lay)
street	**strada, via**	**strah**-dah, **vee**-ah
bridge	**ponte**	**pohn**-tay
tunnel	**tunnel**	**toon**-nel
highway	**autostrada**	ow-toh-**strah**-dah
freeway	**superstrada**	soo-pehr-**strah**-dah
north / south	**nord / sud**	nord / sood
east / west	**est / ovest**	ayst / **oh**-vehst

As in any country, the flashing lights of a patrol car are a sure sign that someone's in trouble. If it's you, say: *"Mi dispiace, sono un turista."* (Sorry, I'm a tourist.) Or, for an unforgettable experience, say: *"Se non le piace come guido, si tolga dal marciapiede."* (If you don't like how I drive, stay off the sidewalk.)

Reading road signs:

alt / stop	stop
carabinieri	police
centro, centrocittà	to the center of town
circonvallazione	ring road
dare la precedenza	yield
deviazione	detour
entrata	entrance
lavori in corso	road work ahead
prossima uscita	next exit
rallentare	slow down
senso unico	one-way street
tutti le (altre) destinazioni	to all (other) destinations
uscita	exit
zona pedonale	pedestrian zone

TRANSPORTATION

Here are the standard symbols you'll see:

DUH	NO ENTRY FOR CARS	ALL VEHICLES PROHIBITED	NO ENTRY	SPEED LIMIT (IN KM)	YIELD	NO PASSING	DANGER	PARKING

Other signs you may bump into:

acqua non potabile	undrinkable water
affittasi, in affitto	for rent or for hire
aperto	open
aperto da... a...	open from... to...
attenzione	caution
bagno, gabinetto, toilette, toletta, WC	toilet
cagnaccio	mean dog
camere libere	vacancy
chiuso	closed
chiuso per ferie	closed for vacation
chiuso per restauro	closed for restoration
completo	no vacancy
donne	women
entrata libera	free admission
entrata vietata	no entry
fuori de servizio / guasto	out of service
non toccare	do not touch
occupato	occupied
parcheggio vietato	no parking
pericolo	danger
proibito	prohibited
saldo	sale
sciopero	on strike
signore	women
signori	men
spingere / tirare	push / pull
torno subito	I'll return soon (sign on store)
uomini	men
uscita d'emergenza	emergency exit
vendesi, in vendita	for sale
vietato	forbidden
vietato fumare	no smoking
vietato l'accesso	keep out

Sleeping

Places to stay:

hotel	**hotel, albergo**	**oh**-tehl, ahl-**behr**-goh
small hotel (usually family-run)	**pensione, locanda**	payn-seeoh-nay, loh-**kahn**-dah
rooms for rent	**affita camere**	ah-**fee**-tah **kah**-may-ray
youth hostel	**ostello della gioventù**	oh-**stehl**-loh **dehl**-lah joh-vehn-**too**
vacancy	**camere libere**	**kah**-may-rah **lee**-bay-ray
no vacancy	**completo**	kohm-**play**-toh

Reserving a room:

Impress your friends by reserving a room by phone. If you want to reserve by fax, use the nifty form in the appendix.

Hello.	**Buon giorno.**	bwohn **jor**-noh
Do you speak English?	**Parla inglese?**	**par**-lah een-**glay**-zay
Do you have a room for...?	**Avete una camera per...?**	ah-**vay**-tay **oo**-nah **kah**-may-rah pehr
...one person / two people	**...una persona / due persone**	**oo**-nah pehr-**soh**-nah / **doo**-ay pehr-**soh**-nay
...tonight	**...stanotte**	stah-**not**-tay
...two nights	**...due notti**	**doo**-ay **not**-tee
...this Friday	**...venerdì**	vay-nehr-**dee**
...June 21	**...il ventuno di giugno**	eel vayn-**too**-noh dee **joon**-yoh

SLEEPING

Yes or no?	**Si o no?**	see oh noh
I'd like...	**Vorrei...**	vor-**rehee**
...a private bathroom.	**...un bagno completo.**	oon **bahn**-yoh kohm-**play**-toh
...your cheapest room.	**...la camera più economica.**	lah **kah**-may-rah pew ay-koh-**noh**-mee-kah
...___ bed (beds)	**...___ letto (letti)**	___ **leht**-toh (**leht**-tee)
for ___ people	**per ___ persone**	pehr ___ pehr-**soh**-nay
in ___ room (rooms).	**nella ___ camera (camere).**	**nay**-lah ___ **kah**-may-rah (**kah**-may-ray)
How much is it?	**Quanto costa?**	**kwahn**-toh **kos**-tah
Anything cheaper?	**Niente di più economico?**	nee-**ehn**-tay dee pew ay-koh-**noh**-mee-koh
I'll take it.	**La prendo.**	lah **prehn**-doh
My name is...	**Mi chiamo...**	mee keeah-moh
I'll stay / We'll stay...	**Starò / Staremo...**	stah-**roh** / stah-**ray**-moh
...for ___ night (nights).	**...per ___ notte (notti).**	pehr ___ **not**-tay (**not**-tee)
I'll come / We'll come...	**Arriverò / Arriveremo...**	ah-ree-vay-**roh** / ah-ree-vay-**ray**-moh
...in one hour.	**...tra un'ora.**	trah oon-**oh**-rah
...before 16:00.	**...prima delle sedici.**	**pree**-mah **dehl**-lay **say**-dee-chee
...Friday before 6 p.m.	**...venerdí prima le sei di sera.**	vay-nehr-**dee pree**-mah lay **seh**ee dee **say**-rah
Thank you.	**Grazie.**	**graht**-seeay

Getting specific:

I'd like a room...	**Vorrei una camera...**	vor-**rehee oo**-nah **kah**-may-rah

...with / without / and	...con / senza / e	kohn / **sehn**-sah / ay
...toilet	...toilette	twah-**leht**-tay
...shower	...doccia	**doh**-chah
...shower down the hall	...doccia in fondo al corridoio	**doh**-chah een **fohn**-doh ahl kor-ree-**doh**-yoh
...bathtub	...vasca da bagno	**vah**-skah dah **bahn**-yoh
...double bed	...letto matrimoniale	**leht**-toh mah-tree-moh-neeah-lay
...twin beds	...letti singoli	**leht**-tee **seeng** goh-lee
...balcony	...balcone	bahl-**koh**-nay
...view	...vista	vee-stah
...only a sink	...solo un lavandino	**soh**-loh oon lah-vahn-**dee**-noh
...on the ground floor	...al piano terreno	ahl peeah-noh tay-**ray**-noh
...television	...televisione	tay-lay-vee-zeeoh-nay
...telephone	...telefono	tay-**lay**-foh-noh
Is there an elevator?	C'è un ascensore?	cheh oon ah-shayn-**soh**-ray
We arrive Monday, depart Wednesday.	Arriviamo lunedì, ripartiamo mercoledì.	ah-ree-veeah-moh loo-nay-dee, ree-par-teeah-moh mehr-koh-lay-**dee**
I'll sleep anywhere. I'm desperate.	Posso dormire ovunque. Sono disperato[a].	**pos**-soh dor-**mee**-ray oh-**voon**-kway. **soh**-noh dee-spay-**rah**-toh
I have a sleeping bag.	Ho un sacco a pelo.	oh oon **sah**-koh ah **pay**-loh
Will you call another hotel?	Chiamerebbe un altro albergo?	keeah-may-**reh**-bay oon **ahl**-troh ahl-**behr**-goh

Confirming, changing, and canceling reservations:
Use this template for your telephone call.

I have a reservation.	**Ho una prenotazione.**	oh **oo**-nah pray-noh-taht-see**oh**-nay
My name is...	**Mi chiamo...**	mee kee**ah**-moh
I'd like to... my reservation.	**Vorrei fare...** **una prenotazione.**	vor-**rehee** **fah**-ray... **oo**-nah pray-noh-taht-see**oh**-nay
...confirm	**...confermare**	kohn-fehr-**mah**-ray
...reconfirm	**...riconfermare**	ree-kohn-fehr-**mah**-ray
...cancel	**...annullare**	ah-noo-**lah**-ray
...change	**...cambiare**	kahm-bee-**ah**-ray
The reservation is / was for...	**La prenotazione** **è / era per...**	lah pray-noh-taht-see**oh**-nay eh / **ehr**-ah pehr
...one person / two people	**...una persona /** **due persone**	**oo**-nah pehr-**soh**-nah / **doo**-ay pehr-**soh**-nay
...today / tomorrow	**...oggi / domani**	**oh**-jee / doh-**mah**-nee
...August 13	**...il tredice di agosto**	eel **tray**-dee-chee dee ah-**goh**-stoh
...one night / two nights	**...una notte / due notti**	**oo**-nah **not**-tay / **doo**-ay **not**-tee
Can you find my reservation?	**Può trovare la** **mia prenotazione?**	pwoh troh-**vah**-ray lah **mee**-ah pray-noh-taht-see**oh**-nay
I'd like to arrive instead on...	**Invece vorrei** **arrivare...**	een-**vay**-chay voh-**rehee** ah-ree-**vah**-ray
Is everything O.K.?	**Va bene?**	vah **behn**-ay

| Thank you. I'll see you then. | **Grazie. Ci vediamo al mio arrivo.** | **graht**-seeay chee vay-deeah-moh ahl **mee**-oh ah-**ree**-voh |
| I'm sorry I need to cancel. | **Mi dispiace ma devo annullare.** | mee dee-speeah-chay mah **day**-voh ah-noo-**lah**-ray |

Nailing down the price:

How much is...?	**Quanto costa...?**	**kwahn**-toh **kos**-tah
...a room for ___ people	**...una camera per ___ persone**	oo-nah **kah**-may-rah pehr ___ pehr-**soh**-nay
...your cheapest room	**...la camera più economica**	lah **kah**-may-rah pew ay-koh-**noh**-mee-kah
Is breakfast included?	**La colazione è inclusa?**	lah koh-laht-seeoh-nay eh een-**kloo**-zah
Is breakfast required?	**È obbligatoria la colazione?**	eh oh-blee-gah-**toh**-reeah lah koh-laht-seeoh-nay
How much without breakfast?	**Quant'è senza la colazione?**	kwahn-**teh sehn**-sah lah koh-laht-seeoh-nay
Complete price?	**Prezzo completo?**	**preht**-soh kohm-**play**-toh
Is it cheaper if I pay cash?	**È più economico se pago in contanti?**	eh pew ay-koh-**noh**-mee-koh **pah**-goh een kohn-**tahn**-tee
Is it cheaper if I stay ___ nights?	**È più economico se mi fermo ___ notti?**	eh pew ay-koh-**noh**-mee-koh say mee **fehr**-moh ___ **not**-tee
I will stay ___ nights.	**Mi fermo ___ notti.**	mee **fehr**-moh ___ **not**-tee

Italian hotels almost always have larger rooms to fit three to six people. Your price per person plummets as you pack more into a room. Breakfasts are usually basic (coffee, rolls and marmalade) and expensive ($6 to $8). They're often optional.

Choosing a room:

Can I see the room?	**Posso vedere la camera?**	**pos**-soh vay-**day**-ray lah **kah**-may-rah
Show me another room?	**Mi mostri un'altra camera?**	mee **moh**-stree oo-**nahl**-trah **kah**-may-rah
Do you have something...?	**Avete qualcosa...?**	ah-**vay**-tay kwahl-**koh**-zah
...larger / smaller	**...di più grande / di più piccolo**	dee pew **grahn**-day / dee pew **pee**-koh-loh
...better / cheaper	**...di meglio / più economico**	dee **mehl**-yoh / pew ay-koh-**noh**-mee-koh
...brighter	**...più luminoso**	pew loo-mee-**noh**-zoh
...in the back	**...nella parte di dietro**	**nay**-lah **par**-tay dee dee**ay**-troh
...quieter	**...di più tranquillo**	dee pew trahn-**kwee**-loh
I'll take it.	**La prendo.**	lah **prehn**-doh
My key, please.	**La mia chiave, per favore.**	lah **mee**-ah kee**ah**-vay pehr fah-**voh**-ray
Sleep well.	**Sogni d'oro.**	**sohn**-yee **doh**-roh
Good night.	**Buona notte.**	**bwoh**-nah **not**-tay

Hotel help:

I'd like...	**Vorrei...**	vor-**rehee**
...a / another	**...un / un altro**	oon / oon **ahl**-troh
...towel.	**...asciugamano.**	ah-shoo-gah-**mah**-noh
...pillow.	**...cuscino.**	koo-**shee**-noh
...clean sheets.	**...lenzuola pulite.**	lehnt-**soooh**-lah poo-**lee**-tay
...blanket.	**...coperta.**	koh-**pehr**-tah
...glass.	**...bicchiere.**	bee-**keeay**-ray
...sink stopper.	**...tappo.**	**tah**-poh
...soap.	**...sapone.**	sah-**poh**-nay
...toilet paper.	**...carta igienica.**	**kar**-tah ee-**jay**-nee-kah
...crib.	**...culla.**	**koo**-lah
...small extra bed.	**...extra letto singolo.**	**ehk**-strah **leht**-toh **seeng**-goh-loh
...different room.	**...altra camera.**	**ahl**-trah **kah**-may-rah
...silence.	**...silenzio.**	see-**lehnt**-seeoh
Where can I...?	**Dove posso...?**	**doh**-vay **pos**-soh
...wash my laundry	**...fare del bucato**	**fah**-ray dayl boo-**kah**-toh
...hang my laundry	**...stendere il bucato**	**stehn**-day-ray eel boo-**kah**-toh
I'd like to stay another night.	**Vorrei fermarmi un'altra notte.**	vor-**rehee** fehr-**mar**-mee oo-**nahl**-trah **not**-tay
Where can I park?	**Dove posso parcheggiare?**	**doh**-vay **pos**-soh par-kay-**jah**-ray
When do you lock up?	**A che ora chiude?**	ah kay **oh**-rah keeoo-day
What time is breakfast?	**A che ora è la colazione?**	ah kay **oh**-rah eh lah koh-laht-**seeoh**-nay

SLEEPING

| Please wake me at 7:00. | **Mi svegli alle sette, per favore.** | mee **zvayl**-yee **ah**-lay **seht**-tay pehr fah-**voh**-ray |

Hotel hassles:

Come with me.	**Venga con me.**	**vayn**-gah kohn may
I have a problem in my room.	**Ho un problema con la mia camera.**	oh oon proh-**blay**-mah kohn lah **mee**-ah **kah**-may-rah
bad odor	**cattivo odore**	kah-**tee**-voh oh-**doh**-ray
bugs	**insetti**	een-**seht**-tee
mice	**topi**	**top**-ee
prostitutes	**prostitute**	proh-stee-**too**-tay
The bed is too soft / hard.	**Il letto è troppo morbido / duro.**	eel **leht**-toh eh **trop**-poh **mor**-bee-doh / **doo**-roh
I'm covered with bug bites.	**Sono pieno[a] di punture di insetti.**	**soh**-noh peeay-noh dee poon-**too**-ray dee een-**seht**-tee
Lamp...	**Lampada...**	lahm-**pah**-dah
Lightbulb...	**Lampadina...**	lahm-pah-**dee**-nah
Electrical outlet...	**Presa...**	**pray**-zah
Key...	**Chiave...**	keeah-vay
Lock...	**Serratura...**	say-rah-**too**-rah
Window...	**Finestra...**	fee-**nay**-strah
Faucet...	**Rubinetto...**	roo-bee-**nay**-toh
Sink...	**Lavabo...**	**lah**-vah-boh
Toilet...	**Toilette...**	twah-**leht**-tay
Shower...	**Doccia...**	**doh**-chah
...doesn't work.	**...non funziona.**	nohn foont-seeoh-nah

There is no hot water.	**Non c'è acqua calda.**	nohn cheh **ah**-kwah **kahl**-dah
When is the water hot?	**A che ora è calda l'acqua?**	ah kay **oh**-rah eh **kahl**-dah **lah**-kwah

Checking out:

I'll leave / We'll leave...	**Parto / Partiamo...**	**par**-toh / par-teeah-moh
...today / tomorrow.	**...oggi / domani.**	**oh**-jee / doh-**mah**-nee
...very early.	**...molto presto.**	**mohl**-toh **prehs**-toh
When is check-out time?	**A che ora devo lasciare la camera?**	ah kay **oh**-rah **day**-voh lah-**shah**-ray lah **kah**-may-rah
Can I pay now?	**Posso pagare subito?**	**pos**-soh pah-**gah**-ray **soo**-bee-toh
The bill, please.	**Il conto, per favore.**	eel **kohn**-toh pehr fah-**voh**-ray
Credit card O.K.?	**Carta di credito è O.K.?**	**kar**-tah dee **kray**-dee-toh eh "O.K."
I slept like a rock.	**Ho dormito come un sasso.**	oh dor-**mee**-toh **koh**-may oon **sah**-soh
Everything was great.	**Tutto magnifico.**	**too**-toh mahn-**yee**-fee-koh
Will you call my next hotel for me?	**Può telefonare a questo altro albergo per me?**	pwoh tay-lay-foh-**nah**-ray ah **kweh**-stoh **ahl**-troh ahl-**behr**-goh pehr may
Can I / Can we...?	**Posso / Possiamo...?**	**pos**-soh / pos-seeah-moh
...leave baggage here until ___	**...lasciare il bagaglio qui fino a ___**	lah-**shah**-ray eel bah-**gahl**-yoh kwee **fee**-noh ah

SLEEPING

Camping:

tent	**tenda**	**tayn**-dah
camping	**campeggio**	kahm-**pay**-joh
Where is the nearest campground?	**Dov'è il campeggio più vicino?**	doh-**veh** eel kahm-**pay**-joh pew vee-**chee**-noh
Can I / Can we...?	**Posso / Possiamo...?**	**pos**-soh / pos-seeah-moh
...camp here for the night	**...campeggiare qui per la notte**	kahm-pay-**jah**-ray kwee pehr lah **not**-tay
Do showers cost extra?	**Costano extra le docce?**	koh-**stah**-noh **ehk**-strah lay **doh**-chay
shower token	**gettone per la doccia**	jeht-**toh**-nay pehr lah **doh**-chay

In some Italian campgrounds and youth hostels, you must buy a *gettone* (token) to activate a coin-operated hot shower. It has a timer inside, like a parking meter. To avoid a sudden cold rinse, buy at least two *gettoni* before getting undressed.

Laundry:

self-service laundry	**lavanderia automatica**	lah-vahn-day-**ree**-ah oh-toh-**mah**-tee-kah
wash	**lavare**	lah-**vah**-ray
dry	**asciugare**	ah-shoo-**gah**-ray
washer	**lavatrice**	lah-vah-**tree**-chay
dryer	**asciugatrice**	ah-shoo-gah-**tree**-chay

detergent	**polvere da bucato**	pohl-**vay**-ray dah boo-**kah**-toh
token	**gettone**	jeht-**toh**-nay
whites / colors	**il bianco / il colore**	eel bee-**ahn**-koh / eel koh-**loh**-ray
delicates	**delicato**	day-lee-**kah**-toh
handwash	**lavare a mano**	lah-**vah**-ray ah **mah**-noh
How does this work?	**Come funziona?**	**koh**-may foont-see-**oh**-nah
Where is the soap?	**Dov'è il sapone?**	doh-**veh** eel sah-**poh**-nay
I need change.	**Ho bisogno di moneta.**	oh bee-**zohn**-yoh dee moh-**nay**-tah
full-service laundry	**lavanderia**	lah-vahn-day-**ree**-ah
Same-day service?	**Servizio in giornata?**	sehr-**veet**-seeoh een jor-**nah**-tah
By when do I need to drop off my clothes?	**Quando devo portare qui i miei panni?**	**kwahn**-doh **day**-voh por-**tah**-ray kwee ee mee-ayee **pah**-nee
When will they be ready?	**Quando saranno pronti?**	**kwahn**-doh sah-**rah**-noh **pron**-tee
Dried?	**Asciutti?**	ah-**shoo**-tee
Folded?	**Piegati?**	peeay-**gah**-tee

SLEEPING

Eating

●Finding a restaurant 55
●Getting a table and menu 53
●The menu 55
●Dietary restrictions 56
●Tableware and condiments 57
●Requests and regrets 58
●Paying 59
●Breakfast 60
●Appetizers and snacks 61
●Pizza and quick meals 62
●Sandwiches 63
●Soups and salads 64
●Pasta 65
●Italian specialties 66
●Seafood 66
●Poultry and meat 67
●How it's prepared 69
●Veggies, beans, and rice 70
●Cheese, fruits and nuts 71
●Just desserts 72
●Drinking 76
  Water, milk, and juice 76
  Coffee and tea 77
  Wine 79
  Beer 80
●Picnicking 82
●Italian-English menu decoder 84

Finding a restaurant:

Where's a good... restaurant?	**Dov'è un buon ristorante...?**	doh-**veh** oon bwohn ree-stoh-**rahn**-tay
...cheap	**...economico**	ay-koh-**noh**-mee-koh
...local-style	**...con cucina casereccia**	kohn koo-**chee**-nah kah-zay-**ray**-chah
...untouristy	**...non per turisti**	nohn pehr too-**ree**-stee
...Chinese	**...cinese**	chee-**nay**-zay
...fast food (Italian-style)	**...tavola calda**	**tah**-voh-lah **kahl**-dah
...cafeteria	**...self-service**	"self-service"
with a salad bar	**con un banco delle insalate**	kohn oon **bahn**-koh **dehl**-lay een-sah-**lah**-tay
with terrace	**con terazza**	kohn tay-**raht**-sah
with candles	**con candele**	kohn kahn-**day**-lay
romantic	**romantico**	roh-**mahn**-tee-koh
moderate price	**a buon mercato**	ah bwohn mer-**kah**-toh
to splurge	**fare sfoggio**	**fah**-ray **sfoh**-joh

Getting a table and menu:

Waiter.	**Cameriere.**	kah-may-reeay-ray
Waitress.	**Cameriera.**	kah-may-reeay-rah
I'd like...	**Vorrei...**	vor-**rehee**
...a table for one / two.	**...un tavolo per uno[a] / due.**	oon **tah**-voh-loh pehr **oo**-noh / **doo**-ay
...non-smoking.	**...non fumatori.**	nohn foo-mah-**toh**-ree
...just a drink.	**...soltanto qualcosa da bere.**	sohl-**tahn**-toh kwahl-**koh**-zah dah **bay**-ray

...a snack.	**...un spuntino.**	oon spoon-**tee**-noh
...just a salad.	**...solo un'insalata.**	**soh**-loh oon-een-sah-**lah**-tah
...only a pasta dish.	**...solo un primo piatto.**	**soh**-loh oon **pree**-moh peeah-toh
...to see the menu.	**...vedere il menù.**	vay-**day**-ray eel may-**noo**
...to order.	**...ordinare.**	or-dee-**nah**-ray
...to eat.	**...mangiare.**	mahn-**jah**-ray
...to pay.	**...pagare.**	pah-**gah**-ray
...to throw up.	**...vomitare.**	voh-mee-**tah**-ray
What do you recommend?	**Che cosa raccomanda?**	kay **koh**-zah rah-koh-**mahn**-dah
What's your favorite?	**Qual'è il suo piatto favorito?**	kwah-**leh** eel **soo**-oh peeah-toh fah-voh-**ree**-toh
Is it ...?	**È...?**	eh
...good	**...buono**	**bwoh**-noh
...expensive	**...caro**	**kah**-roh
...light	**...leggero**	lay-**jay**-roh
...filling	**...sostanzioso**	soh-stahnt-seeoh-zoh
What is that?	**Che cosa è quello?**	kay **koh**-zah eh **kway**-loh
What is...?	**Che cosa c'è...?**	kay **koh**-zah cheh
...local	**...di locale**	dee loh-**kah**-lay
...fast	**...di veloce**	dee vay-**loh**-chay
...cheap and filling	**...di economico e sostanzioso**	dee ay-koh-**noh**-mee-koh ay soh-stahnt-seeoh-zoh
Do you have...?	**Avete...?**	ah-**vay**-tay
...an English menu	**...un menù in inglese**	oon may-**noo** een een-**glay**-zay
...children's portions	**...le porzioni per bambini**	lay port-seeoh-nee pehr bahm-**bee**-nee

The menu:

menu	**menù**	may-**noo**
menu of the day	**menù del giorno**	may-**noo** dayl **jor**-noh
tourist menu	**menù turistico**	may-**noo** too-**ree**-stee-koh
specialty of the house	**specialità della casa**	spay-chah-lee-**tah dehl**-lah **kah**-zah
breakfast	**colazione**	koh-laht-**seeoh**-nay
lunch	**pranzo**	**prahnt**-soh
dinner	**cena**	**chay**-nah
appetizers	**antipasti**	ahn-tee-**pah**-stee
bread	**pane**	**pah**-nay
salad	**insalata**	een-sah-**lah**-tah
soup	**minestra, zuppa**	mee-**nehs**-trah, **tsoo**-pah
first course (pasta, soup)	**primo piatto**	**pree**-moh peeah-toh
main course (meat, fish)	**secondo piatto**	say-**kohn**-doh peeah-toh
meat	**carni**	**kar**-nee
poultry	**pollame**	poh-**lah**-may
seafood	**frutti di mare**	**froo**-tee dee **mah**-ray
side dishes	**contorni**	kohn-**tor**-nee
vegetables	**legumi**	lay-**goo**-mee
cheeses	**formaggi**	for-**mah**-jee
desserts	**dolci**	**dohl**-chee
beverages	**bevande, bibite**	bay-**vahn**-day, **bee**-bee-tay
beer	**birra**	**beer**-rah
wines	**vini**	**vee**-nee
cover charge	**coperto**	koh-**pehr**-toh

EATING

service (not) included	**servizio (non) incluso**	sehr-**veet**-seeoh (nohn) een-**kloo**-zoh
with / and /	**con / e /**	kohn / ay /
or / without	**o / senza**	oh / **sehn**-sah

Pay attention to the money-saving words in this chapter. Without them, Italy is a very expensive place to eat. Most menus explain the *servizio* (service) charge which will be added to your bill along with the *coperto* (cover charge).

Budget eaters do best in places with no or minimal service and cover charges, and by sticking to the *primo piatto* (first course dishes). A hearty *minestrone* and/or *pasta* fills the average American. Pricier restaurants are wise to this, and some don't allow you to eat without ordering the expensive *secondo* course.

Often a good deal, a *menù del giorno* (menu of the day) offers you a choice of appetizer, entrée, and dessert (or wine) at a fixed price.

Dietary restrictions:

I'm allergic to...	**Sono allergico[a] al...**	**soh**-noh ahl-**lehr**-jee-koh ahl
I cannot eat...	**Non posso mangiare...**	nohn **pos**-soh mahn-**jah**-ray
...dairy products.	**...latticini.**	lah-tee-**chee**-nee
...meat / pork.	**...carne / maiale.**	**car**-nay / mah-**yah**-lay
...salt / sugar.	**...sale / zucchero.**	**sah**-lay / **tsoo**-kay-roh
I am diabetic.	**Ho il diabete.**	oh eel deeah-**bay**-tay
No fat.	**Senza grassi.**	**sehn**-sah **grah**-see

Minimal fat.	**Pochi grassi.**	**poh**-kee **grah**-see
Low cholesterol.	**Basso colesterolo.**	**bah**-soh koh-lay-stay-**roh**-loh
No caffeine.	**Senza caffeina.**	**sehn**-sah kah-fayee-nah
No alcohol.	**Niente alcool.**	neeee**hn**-tay **ahl**-kohl
I am a...	**Sono un...**	**soh**-noh oon
...vegetarian.	**...vegetariano[a].**	vay-jay-tah-ree**ah**-noh
...strict vegetarian.	**...strettamente vegetariano[a].**	stray-tah-**mayn**-tay vay-jay-tah-ree**ah**-noh
...carnivore.	**...carnivoro[a].**	kar-**nee**-voh-roh
...big eater.	**...mangione.**	mahn-jee**oh**-nay

Tableware and condiments:

plate	**piatto**	peeah-toh
extra plate	**un altro piatto**	oon **ahl**-troh peeah-toh
napkin	**tovagliolo**	toh-vahl-**yoh**-loh
silverware	**posate**	poh-**zah**-tay
knife	**coltello**	kohl-**tehl**-loh
fork	**forchetta**	for-**kay**-tah
spoon	**cucchiaio**	koo-kee**ah**-yoh
cup	**tazza**	**taht**-sah
glass	**bicchiere**	bee-kee**eay**-ray
carafe	**caraffa**	kah-**rah**-fah
water	**acqua**	**ah**-kwah
bread	**pane**	**pah**-nay
breadsticks	**grissini**	gree-**see**-nee
butter	**burro**	**boo**-roh
margarine	**margarina**	mar-gah-**ree**-nah
toothpick	**stuzzicadente**	stoot-see-kah-**dehn**-tay
salt / pepper	**sale / pepe**	**sah**-lay / **pay**-pay
sugar	**zucchero**	**tsoo**-kay-roh
artificial sweetener	**dolcificante**	dohl-chee-fee-**kahn**-tay

honey	**miele**	meeay-lay
mustard	**senape**	say-nah-pay
mayonnaise	**maionese**	mah-yoh-nay-zay

Restaurant requests and regrets:

A little.	**Un po.'**	oon poh
More.	**Un altro po.'**	oon ahl-troh poh
Another.	**Un altro.**	oon ahl-troh
The same.	**Lo stesso.**	loh stehs-soh
I did not order this.	**Io questo non l'ho ordinato.**	eeoh kweh-stoh nohn loh or-dee-nah-toh
Is it included with the meal?	**È incluso nel pasto questo?**	eh een-kloo-zoh nayl pah-stoh kweh-stoh
I'm in a hurry.	**Sono di fretta.**	soh-noh dee fray-tah
I must leave by...	**Devo andare via alle...**	day-voh ah-dah-ray vee-ah ah-lay
When will the food be ready?	**Tra quanto è pronto il cibo?**	trah kwahn-toh eh pron-toh eel chee-boh
I've changed my mind.	**Ho cambiato idea.**	oh kahm-beeah-toh ee-day-ah
Can I get it "to go"?	**Posso averlo da portar via?**	pos-soh ah-vehr-loh dah por-tar vee-ah
This is...	**Questo è...**	kweh-stoh eh
...dirty.	**...sporco.**	spor-koh
...greasy.	**...grasso.**	grah-soh
...too salty.	**...troppo salato.**	trop-poh sah-lah-toh
...undercooked.	**...troppo crudo.**	trop-poh kroo-doh
...overcooked.	**...troppo cotto.**	trop-poh kot-toh
...inedible.	**...immangiabile.**	eem-mahn-jah-bee-lay

...cold.	...freddo.	**fray**-doh
Heat it up?	**Lo può scaldare?**	loh pwoh skahl-**dah**-ray
Enjoy your meal!	**Buon appetito!**	bwohn ah-pay-**tee**-toh
Enough.	**Basta.**	**bah**-stah
Finished.	**Finito.**	fee-**nee**-toh
Do any of your customers return?	**Ritornano i vostri clienti?**	ree-**tor**-nah-noh ee **voh**-stree klee-**ehn**-tee
Yuck!	**Che schifo!**	kay **skee**-foh
Delicious!	**Delizioso!**	day-leet-**seeoh**-zoh
Divinely good!	**Una vera bontà!**	**oo**-nah **vay**-rah bohn-**tah**
My compliments to the chef!	**Complimenti al cuoco!**	kohm-plee-**mayn**-tee ahl **koooh**-koh

Paying for your meal:

The bill, please.	**Il conto, per favore.**	eel **kohn**-toh pehr fah-**voh**-ray
Together.	**Conto unico.**	**kohn**-toh **oo**-nee-koh
Separate checks.	**Conto separato.**	**kohn**-toh say-pah-**rah**-toh
Credit card O.K.?	**Carta di credito è O.K.?**	**kar**-tah dee **kray**-dee-toh eh "O.K."
Is there a cover charge?	**Si paga per il coperto?**	see **pah**-gah pehr eel koh-**pehr**-toh
Is service included?	**È incluso il servizio?**	eh een-**kloo**-zoh eel sehr-**veet**-seeoh
This is not correct.	**Questo non è giusto.**	**kweh**-stoh nohn eh **joo**-stoh
Explain it?	**Lo può spiegare?**	loh pwoh speeay-**gah**-ray
What if I wash the dishes?	**E se lavassi i piatti?**	ay say lah-**vah**-see ee pee**ah**-tee

Keep the change.	**Tenga il resto.**	**tayn**-gah eel **rehs**-toh
This is for you.	**Questo è per lei.**	**kweh**-stoh eh pehr **leh**ee

In Italian bars and freeway rest stops, pay first at the *cassa* (cash register), then take your receipt to the counter to get your food. In restaurants, you'll get the bill only when you ask for it. Summon your waiter's attention by saying, *"Per favore"* (please). The menu will state if the *servizio* (tip) is included. Tipping beyond this is not expected, but it's polite to round up the bill. If the service has been super, toss in an extra euro per person at your table.

Breakfast:

breakfast	**colazione**	koh-laht-see**oh**-nay
bread	**pane**	**pah**-nay
roll	**brioche**	bree-**osh**
toast	**toast**	tost
butter	**burro**	**boo**-roh
jam	**marmellata**	mar-mehl-**lah**-tah
jelly	**gelatina**	jay-lah-**tee**-nah
pastry	**pasticcini**	pah-stee-**chee**-nee
croissant	**cornetto**	kor-**nay**-toh
omelet	**omelette, frittata**	oh-may-**leht**-tay, free-**tah**-tah
eggs...	**uova...**	**woh**-vah
...fried / scrambled	**...fritte / strapazzate**	**free**-tay / strah-paht-**sah**-tay
boiled egg...	**uovo alla coque...**	**woh**-voh **ah**-lah kok
...soft / hard	**...molle / sodo**	**mol**-lay / **soh**-doh
ham	**prosciutto cotto**	proh-**shoo**-toh **kot**-toh

cheese	**formaggio**	for-**mah**-joh
yogurt	**yogurt**	**yoh**-goort
cereal (any kind)	**corn flex**	korn flehx
milk	**latte**	**lah**-tay
hot chocolate	**cioccolata calda**	choh-koh-**lah**-tah **kahl**-dah
fruit juice	**succo di frutta**	**soo**-koh dee **froo**-tah
fresh orange juice	**spremuta di arancia**	spray-**moo**-tah dee ah-**rahn**-chah
coffee / tea (see Drinking)	**caffè / tè**	kah-**feh** / teh
Is breakfast included (in the room cost)?	**La colazione è inclusa?**	lah koh-laht-see**oh**-nay eh een-**kloo**-zah

EATING

Italian breakfasts, like Italian bath towels, are small: coffee and a roll with butter and marmalade. The strong coffee is often mixed about half and half with milk. At your hotel, refills are usually free. The delicious red orange juice is made from Sicilian blood oranges (*arancia tarocco*). Local open-air markets thrive in the morning, and a picnic breakfast followed by a *cappuccino* in a bar is a good option.

Appetizers and snacks:

antipasto misto	mixed appetizers (usually meat)
bruschetta	toast with tomatoes and garlic
crostini alla Fiorentina	toast with liver paté
crostini alla Napoletana	toast with cheese
formaggi misti	assorted cheeses
prosciutto e melone	cured ham with melon

salame	cured pork sausage
salumi misti	assortment of meats
toast al prosciutto e formaggio	toast with ham and cheese

Pizza and quick meals:

Pizza Rustica shops offer a fast, cheap, hot meal, selling pizza by the slice (*pezzo*) or weight (*etto* = 100 grams = a quarter pound). *Due etti* (200 grams) make a good light lunch. Eat your pizza on the spot or order it *"Da portar via"* (for the road). To get cold pizza warmed up, say, *"Calda, per favore"* (Hot, please). To get an extra plate, ask for a *"un altro piatto."* Pizza words include:

acciughe	anchovies
alla diavola	spicy
calzone	folded pizza with various fillings
capricciosa	ham, mushrooms, olives, and artichokes
carciofini	artichokes
ciaccino	"white" pizza (no tomato sauce)
frutti di mare	seafood (shrimp, squid, mussels)
funghi	mushrooms
Maialona	ham, sausage and hot dogs
Margherita	cheese and tomato sauce
marinara	tomato, garlic and oregano
melanzane	eggplant
Napoletana	cheese, anchovies and tomato sauce
peperoni	green or red peppers (not sausage!)
porcini	porcini mushrooms
prosciutto	ham
Quattro Stagioni	4 toppings on separate quarters of a pizza

salamino piccante	pepperoni	
salsiccia	sausage	
wurstel	hot dogs	

For other quick, tasty meals, drop by a *Rosticceria*—a deli where you'll find a cafeteria-style display of reasonably priced food. Get it "to go" or take a seat and eat.

Sandwiches:

sandwiches	**panini**	pah-**nee**-nee
small sandwiches	**tramezzini**	trah-mehd-**zee**-nee
I'd like a sandwich.	**Vorrei un panino.**	vor-**rehee** oon pah-**nee**-noh
cheese	**formaggio**	for-**mah**-joh
tuna	**tonno**	**toh**-noh
chicken	**pollo**	**poh**-loh
turkey	**tacchino**	tah-**kee**-noh
ham	**prosciutto**	proh-**shoo**-toh
salami	**salame**	sah-**lah**-may
egg salad	**insalata con uova**	een-sah-**lah**-tah kohn **woh**-vah
lettuce	**lattuga**	lah-**too**-gah
tomatoes	**pomodori**	poh-moh-**doh**-ree
onions	**cipolle**	chee-**poh**-lay
mustard	**senape**	say-**nah**-pay
mayonnaise	**maionese**	mah-yoh-**nay**-zay

In many bars, *tramezzini* (small sandwiches) are sold ready-made. The price is usually posted. First pay the cashier for the sandwich (and coffee or whatever), then give your receipt to the person behind the bar to get your food. Two or three sandwiches make an easy, fast meal.

EATING

Soups and salads:

soup	minestra, zuppa	mee-**nehs**-trah, **tsoo**-pah
soup of the day	zuppa del giorno	**tsoo**-pah dayl **jor**-noh
broth...	brodo...	**brod**-oh
...chicken	...di pollo	dee **poh**-loh
...beef	...di carne	dee **kar**-nay
...vegetable	...di verdura	dee vehr-**doo**-rah
...with noodles	...con pastina	kohn pah-**stee**-nah
...with rice	...con riso	kohn **ree**-zoh
vegetable soup	minestrone	mee-nay-**stroh**-nay
green salad	insalata verde	een-sah-**lah**-tah **vehr**-day
mixed salad	insalata mista	een-sah-**lah**-tah **mee**-stah
seafood salad	insalata di mare	een-sah-**lah**-tah dee **mah**-ray
chef's salad...	insalata dello chef...	een-sah-**lah**-tah **dehl**-loh shehf
...with ham and cheese	...con prosciutto e formaggio	kohn proh-**shoo**-toh ay for-**mah**-joh
...with egg	...con uova	kohn **woh**-vah
lettuce	lattuga	lah-**too**-gah
tomatoes	pomodori	poh-moh-**doh**-ree
cucumber	cetrioli	chay-tree**oh**-lee
oil / vinegar	olio / aceto	**oh**-leeoh / ah-**chay**-toh
tray with oil & vinegar	oliera	oh-lee-**ehr**-ah
What is in this salad?	Che cosa c'è in questa insalata?	kay **koh**-zah cheh een **kweh**-stah een-sah-**lah**-tah

In Italian restaurants, salad dressing is normally just the oil and vinegar at the table (if it's missing, ask for the *oliera*). Salad bars at fast food restaurants and *autostrada* rest stops can be a good budget bet.

Pasta:

Italy is the land of *pasta.* You can taste over 500 types! While there are a few differences in ingredients, the big deal is basically the shape. Watch for *rigatone* (little tubes), *canneloni* (big tubes), *fettucine* (thin, flat noodles), *farfalline* (butterfly-shaped pasta), *gnocchi* (shell-shaped noodles made from potatoes), *liguine* (flat noodles), *penne* (angle-cut tubes), *rotelline* (wheel-shaped pasta), *tagliatelle* (short, flat noodles), and *tortellini* (pasta "doughnuts" filled with meat or cheese), and surprise...*spaghetti.* Pasta can be stuffed *ravoli*-style with various meats, cheeses, herbs, and spices. Pasta sauces and styles include:

amatriciana	Roman-style with bacon, tomato, & spices
bolognese	meat & tomato sauce
carbonara	bacon, egg, cheese, & pepper
genovese	pesto
in brodo	in broth
marinara	tomato & garlic
panna	cream
pescatora	seafood
pesto	olive oil, garlic, pine nuts, & basil
pomodoro	tomato only
quattro formaggi	four cheeses
ragù	meaty tomato sauce
sugo	sauce, usually tomato
vongole	with clams & spices

Italian specialities:

cozze ripiene	mussels stuffed with bread, cheese, garlic, & tomatoes
focaccia	flat bread with herbs
insalata caprese	salad of mozzarella, tomatoes, & basil
pancetta	thick bacon
polenta	moist cornmeal (Venice)
ribollita	cabbage & bean soup (Tuscany)
risotto	rice dish with meat, seafood, or vegetables (Northern Italy)
saltimbocca	veal wrapped in ham (Rome)
tramezzini	crustless filled sandwiches

Seafood:

seafood	**frutti di mare**	**froo**-tee dee **mah**-ray
assorted seafood	**misto di frutti di mare**	**mee**-stoh dee **froo**-tee dee **mah**-ray
assorted deep-fried seafood	**fritto misto**	**free**-toh **mee**-stoh
fish	**pesce**	**peh**-shay
cod	**merluzzo**	mehr-**loot**-soh
salmon	**salmone**	sahl-**moh**-nay
sole	**sogliola**	sohl-**yoh**-lah
trout	**trota**	**trot**-ah
tuna	**tonno**	**toh**-noh
herring	**aringa**	ah-**reeng**-gah
sardines	**sardine**	sar-**dee**-nay

anchovies	**acciughe**	ah-**choo**-gay
clams	**vongole**	**vohn**-goh-lay
mussels	**cozze**	**kot**-say
oysters	**ostriche**	**os**-tree-kay
shrimp	**gamberetti**	gahm-bay-**ray**-tee
prawns	**scampi**	**skahm**-pee
crab	**granchio**	**grahn**-keeoh
lobster	**aragosta**	ah-rah-**goh**-stah
squid	**calamari**	kah-lah-**mah**-ree
Where did this live?	**Da dove viene questo?**	dah **doh**-vay veeay-nay **kweh**-stoh
Just the head, please.	**Solo la testa, per favore.**	**soh**-loh lah **tehs**-tah pehr fah-**voh**-ray

Poultry and meat:

poultry	**pollame**	poh-**lah**-may
chicken	**pollo**	**poh**-loh
turkey	**tacchino**	tah-**kee**-noh
duck	**anatra**	**ah**-nah-trah
meat	**carne**	**kar**-nay
beef	**manzo**	**mahnd**-zoh
roast beef	**roast beef**	"roast beef"
beef steak	**bistecca di manzo**	bee-**stay**-kah dee **mahnd**-zoh
porterhouse steak (thick and rare)	**bistecca Fiorentina**	bee-**stay**-kah fee-oh-rehn-**tee**-nah
sirloin steak	**entrecote**	ayn-tray-**koh**-tay
meat stew	**stufato di carne**	stoo-**fah**-toh dee **kar**-nay

veal	**vitello**	vee-**tehl**-loh
thin-sliced veal	**scaloppine**	skah-loh-**pee**-nay
cutlet (veal)	**cotoletta**	koh-toh-**lay**-tah
pork	**maiale**	mah-**yah**-lay
cured ham	**prosciutto crudo**	proh-**shoo**-toh **kroo**-doh
cooked ham	**prosciutto cotto**	proh-**shoo**-toh **kot**-toh
sausage	**salsiccia**	sahl-**see**-chah
lamb	**agnello**	ahn-**yehl**-loh
bunny	**coniglio**	koh-**neel**-yoh
brains	**cervella**	chehr-**vehl**-lah
sweetbreads	**animelle di vitello**	ah-nee-**mehl**-lay dee vee-**tehl**-loh
tongue	**lingua**	**leeng**-gwah
liver	**fegato**	**fay**-gah-toh
tripe	**trippa**	**tree**-pah
How long has this been dead?	**Da quanto tempo è morto questo?**	dah **kwahn**-toh **tehm**-poh eh **mor**-toh **kweh**-stoh

Avoiding mis-steaks:

raw	**crudo**	**kroo**-doh
rare	**al sangue**	ahl **sahn**-gway
medium	**cotto**	**kot**-toh
well done	**ben cotto**	bayn **kot**-toh
almost burnt	**quasi bruciato**	**kwah**-zee broo-**chah**-toh

On a menu, the price of steak is often listed per *etto* (100 grams).

How it's prepared:

hot / cold	**caldo / freddo**	**kahl**-doh / **fray**-doh
raw / cooked	**crudo / cotto**	**kroo**-doh / **kot**-toh
assorted	**assortiti**	ah-sor-**tee**-tee
baked	**al forno**	ahl **for**-noh
boiled	**bollito**	boh-**lee**-toh
fillet	**filetto**	fee-**lay**-toh
fresh	**fresco**	**fray**-skoh
fried	**fritto**	**free**-toh
fried with breadcrumbs	**Milanese**	mee-lah-**nay**-zay
grilled	**alla griglia**	**ah**-lah **greel**-yah
homemade	**casalingo**	kah-zah-**leen**-goh
in cream sauce	**con panna**	kohn **pah**-nah
microwave	**forno a micro onde**	**for**-noh ah **mee**-kroh **ohn**-day
mild	**non piccante**	nohn pee-**kahn**-tay
mixed	**misto**	**mee**-stoh
poached	**affogato**	ah-foh-**gah**-toh
roasted	**arrosto**	ah-**roh**-stoh
sautéed	**saltato in padella**	sahl-**tah**-toh een pah-**dehl**-lah
smoked	**affumicato**	ah-foo-mee-**kah**-toh
spicy hot	**piccante**	pee-**kahn**-tay
steamed	**al vapore**	ahl vah-**poh**-ray
stuffed	**ripieno**	ree-peeay-noh
sweet	**dolce**	**dohl**-chay
with cheese and breadcrumbs	**alla Parmigiana**	**ah**-lah par-mee-**jah**-nah

Veggies, beans, and rice:

vegetables	**legumi, verdure**	lay-**goo**-mee, vehr-**doo**-ray
mixed vegetables	**misto di verdure**	**mee**-stoh dee vehr-**doo**-ray
artichoke	**carciofo**	kar-**choh**-foh
asparagus	**asparagi**	ah-spah-**rah**-jee
beans	**fagioli**	fah-**joh**-lee
beets	**barbabietole**	bar-bah-beeay-**toh**-lay
broccoli	**broccoli**	**brok**-koh-lee
cabbage	**verza**	**vehrt**-sah
carrots	**carote**	kah-**rot**-ay
cauliflower	**cavolfiore**	kah-vohl-feeoh-ray
corn	**granturco**	grahn-**toor**-koh
cucumber	**cetrioli**	chay-treeoh-lee
eggplant	**melanzana**	may-lahnt-**sah**-nah
French fries	**patate fritte**	pah-**tah**-tay **free**-tay
garlic	**aglio**	**ahl**-yoh
green beans	**fagiolini**	fah-joh-**lee**-nee
lentils	**lenticchie**	lehn-**tee**-keeay
mushrooms	**funghi**	**foong**-gee
olives	**olive**	oh-**lee**-vay
onions	**cipolle**	chee-**poh**-lay
peas	**piselli**	pee-**zehl**-lee
peppers...	**peperoni...**	pay-pay-**roh**-nee
...green / red	**...verdi / rossi**	**vehr**-dee / **roh**-see
pickles	**cetriolini**	chay-treeoh-**lee**-nee
potatoes	**patate**	pah-**tah**-tay
rice	**riso**	**ree**-zoh
spinach	**spinaci**	spee-**nah**-chee
tomatoes	**pomodori**	poh-moh-**doh**-ree
zucchini	**zucchine**	tsoo-**kee**-nay

Say cheese:

cheese	**formaggio**	for-**mah**-joh
mild and soft	**fresco**	**fray**-skoh
sharp and hard	**stagionato**	stah-joh-**nah**-toh
mozzarella	**mozzarella**	moht-sah-**ray**-lah
small mozzarella balls	**bocconcini de mozzarella**	boh-koh-**chee**-nee dee moht-sah-**ray**-lah
goat	**di capra**	dee **kah**-prah
sheep cheese	**pecorino**	pay-koh-**ree**-noh
bleu cheese	**gorgonzola**	gor-gohnd-**zoh**-lah
cream cheese	**formaggio philadelphia**	for-**mah**-joh fee-lah-**dehl**-feeah
Swiss cheese	**groviera, emmenthal**	groh-veeay-rah, ehm-mehn-**tahl**
parmesan	**parmigiano**	par-mee-**jah**-noh
a soft white cheese	**Bel Paese**	behl pah-**ay**-zay
a tasty spreadable cheese	**stracchino**	strah-**kee**-noh
A little taste?	**Un assaggio?**	oon ah-**sah**-joh

Fruits and nuts:

almond	**mandorle**	mahn-**dor**-lay
apple	**mela**	**may**-lah
apricot	**albicocca**	ahl-bee-**koh**-kah
banana	**banana**	bah-**nah**-nah
berries	**frutti di bosco**	**froo**-tee dee **bos**-koh
canteloupe	**melone**	may-**loh**-nay
cherry	**ciliegia**	chee-leeay-jah
chestnut	**castagne**	kah-**stahn**-yay

coconut	**noce di cocco**	**noh**-chay dee **koh**-koh
dates	**datteri**	**dah**-tay-ree
fig	**fico**	**fee**-koh
fruit	**frutta**	**froo**-tah
grapefruit	**pompelmo**	pohm-**pehl**-moh
grapes	**uva**	**oo**-vah
hazelnut	**nocciola**	noh-**choh**-lah
lemon	**limone**	lee-**moh**-nay
orange	**arancia**	ah-**rahn**-chah
peach	**pesca**	**pehs**-kah
peanuts	**noccioline**	noh-choh-**lee**-nay
pear	**pera**	**pay**-rah
pineapple	**ananas**	**ah**-nah-nahs
pistachio	**pistacchio**	pee-**stah**-keeoh
plum	**susina**	soo-**zee**-nah
prune	**prugna**	**proon**-yah
raspberry	**lampone**	lahm-**poh**-nay
strawberry	**fragola**	**frah**-goh-lah
tangerine	**mandarino**	mahn-dah-**ree**-noh
walnut	**noce**	**noh**-chay
watermelon	**cocomero**	koh-koh-**may**-roh

On a menu, you might see *"frutta fresca di stagione"* (fresh fruit of the season).

Just desserts:

dessert	**dolci**	**dohl**-chee
cake	**torta**	**tor**-tah
ice cream	**gelato**	jay-**lah**-toh
sherbet	**sorbetto**	sor-**bay**-toh
fruit salad	**macedonia**	mah-chay-**doh**-neeah
fruit with ice cream	**coppa di frutta**	**kop**-pah dee **froo**-tah
tart	**tartina**	tar-**tee**-nah
pie	**crostada**	kroh-**stah**-dah

whipped cream	**panna**	**pah**-nah
chocolate mousse	**mousse**	moos
pudding	**budino**	boo-**dee**-noh
pastry	**pasta**	**pah**-stah
strudel	**strudel**	**stroo**-dehl
cookies	**biscotti**	bee-**skot**-tee
candies	**caramelle**	kah-rah-**mehl**-lay
low calorie	**poche calorie**	**poh**-kay kah-loh-**ree**-ay
homemade	**casalingo**	kah-zah-**leen**-goh
Exquisite.	**Squisito.**	skwee-**zee**-toh
Sinfully good.	**Un peccato**	oon pay-**kah**-toh
(a sin of the throat)	**di gola.**	dee **goh**-lah
So good I even licked	**Così buono che**	koh-**zee** bwoh-noh kay
my moustache.	**mi sono leccato[a]**	mee **soh**-noh lay-**kah**-toh
	anche i baffi.	**ahn**-kay ee **bah**-fee

EATING

More Italian treats:

bignè con crema	cream puffs (Florence)
cassata	ice cream, sponge cake, ricotta cheese, fruit, & pistachios (Sicily)
granita	snow-cone
panforte	dense fruit & nut cake (Siena)
tartufo	super-chocolate ice cream (Rome)
tiramisú	espresso-soaked cake with chocolate, cream, & brandy
zabaglione	delicious egg & liquor cream
zuppa inglese	rum-soaked cake with whipped cream

Gelati talk:

cone / cup	**cono / coppa**	**koh**-noh / **kop**-pah
one scoop	**una pallina**	**oo**-nah pah-**lee**-nah
two scoops	**due palline**	**doo**-ay pah-**lee**-nay
with whipped cream	**con panna**	kohn **pah**-nah
A little taste?	**Un assaggio?**	oon ah-**sah**-joh
How many flavors	**Quanti gusti**	**kwahn**-tee **goo**-stee **pos**-soh
can I get per scoop?	**posso avere per pallina?**	ah-**vay**-ray pehr pah-**lee**-nah
apricot	**albicocca**	ahl-bee-**koh**-kah
berries	**frutti di bosco**	**froo**-tee dee **bos**-koh
blueberry	**mirtillo**	meer-**tee**-loh
cantaloupe	**melone**	may-**loh**-nay
chocolate	**cioccolato**	choh-koh-**lah**-toh
vanilla and chocolate chips	**stracciatella**	strah-chah-**tehl**-lah
chocolate hazelnut	**bacio**	**bah**-choh
coffee	**caffè**	kah-**feh**
hazelnut	**nocciola**	noh-**choh**-lah
lemon	**limone**	lee-**moh**-nay
mint	**menta**	**mayn**-tah
orange	**arancia**	ah-**rahn**-chah
peach	**pesca**	**pehs**-kah
pear	**pera**	**pay**-rah
pineapple	**ananas**	**ah**-nah-nahs
raspberry	**lampone**	lahm-**poh**-nay
rice	**riso**	**ree**-zoh
strawberry	**fragola**	**frah**-goh-lah

| super chocolate | **tartufo** | tar-**too**-foh |
| vanilla | **crema** | **kray**-mah |

Bacio (chocolate hazelnut) also means "kiss." *Baci* (kisses) are Italy's version of Chinese fortune cookies. The poetic fortunes, wrapped around chocolate balls, are written by people whose love of romance exceeds their grasp of English.

EATING

Drinking

Water, milk, and juice:

mineral water...	**acqua minerale...**	**ah**-kwah mee-nay-**rah**-lay
...carbonated	**...gassata**	gah-**sah**-tah
...not carbonated	**...non gassata**	nohn gah-**sah**-tah
tap water	**acqua del rubinetto**	**ah**-kwah dayl roo-bee-**nay**-toh
milk...	**latte...**	**lah**-tay
...whole	**...intero**	een-**tay**-roh
...skim	**...magro**	**mah**-groh
...fresh	**...fresco**	**fray**-skoh
milk shake	**frappè**	frah-**peh**
hot chocolate...	**cioccolata calda...**	choh-koh-**lah**-tah **kahl**-dah
...with whipped cream	**...con panna**	kohn **pah**-nah
orange soda	**aranciata**	ah-rahn-**chah**-tah
lemon soda	**limonata**	lee-moh-**nah**-tah
juice...	**succo di...**	**soo**-koh dee
...fruit	**...frutta**	**froo**-tah
...apple	**...mela**	**may**-lah
...apricot	**...albicocca**	ah-bee-**koh**-kah
...grapefruit	**...pompelmo**	pohm-**pehl**-moh
...orange	**...arancia**	ah-**rahn**-chah
...peach	**...pesca**	**pehs**-kah
...pear	**...pera**	**pay**-rah

freshly-squeezed orange juice	**spremuta d'arancia**	spray-**moo**-tah dah-**rahn**-chah
with / without...	**con / senza...**	kohn / **sehn**-sah
...ice / sugar	**...ghiaccio / zucchero**	geeah-choh / **tsoo**-kay-roh
glass / cup	**bicchiere / tazza**	bee-keeay-ray / **taht**-sah
bottle...	**bottiglia...**	boh-**teel**-yah
...small / large	**...piccola / grande**	**pee**-koh-lah / **grahn**-day
Is this water safe to drink?	**È potabile quest'acqua?**	eh poh-**tah**-bee-lay kweh-**stah**-kwah

I drink the tap water in Italy (Venice's is piped in from a mountain spring, and Florence's is very chlorinated), but it's good style and never expensive to order a *litro* (liter) or *mezzo litro* (half liter) of bottled water with your meal.

Coffee and tea:

coffee...	**caffè...**	kah-**feh**
...with water	**...lungo**	**loon**-goh
...with a little milk	**...macchiato**	mah-keeah-toh
...with milk	**...latte**	**lah**-tay
...with whipped cream	**...con panna**	kohn **pah**-nah
...iced	**...freddo**	**fray**-doh
...instant	**...solubile**	soo-**loo**-bee-lay
...American-style	**...Americano**	ah-may-ree-**kah**-noh
coffee with foamy milk	**cappuccino**	kah-poo-**chee**-noh
decaffeinated	**decaffeinato, Hag**	day-kah-fay-**nah**-toh, hahg
black	**nero**	**nay**-roh
milk...	**latte...**	**lah**-tay

EATING

...with a little coffee	**...macchiato**	mah-kee**ah**-toh
sugar	**zucchero**	**tsoo**-kay-roh
hot water	**acqua calda**	**ah**-kwah **kahl**-dah
tea / lemon	**tè / limone**	teh / lee-**moh**-nay
tea bag	**bustina di tè**	boo-**stee**-nah dee teh
herbal tea	**tè deteìnato**	teh day-tay-een-**nah**-toh
iced tea	**tè freddo**	teh **fray**-doh
mint tea	**tè alla menta**	teh **ah**-lah **mehn**-tah
fruit tea	**tè alla frutta**	teh **ah**-lah **froo**-tah
small / large	**piccola / grande**	**pee**-koh-lah / **grahn**-day
Another cup.	**Un'altra tazza.**	oo-**nahl**-trah **taht**-sah
Same price if I sit	**Costa uguale al**	**kos**-tah oo-**gwah**-lay ahl
or stand?	**tavolo o al banco?**	**tah**-voh-loh oh ahl **bahn**-koh

Caffè is espresso served in a teeny tiny cup. Foamy *cappuccino* was named after the monks with their brown robes and frothy cowls. A *corretto* is coffee and firewater. In a bar, you'll pay at the *cassa*, then take your receipt to the person who makes the coffee. Refills are never free, except at hotel breakfasts.

When you're ordering coffee in bars in bigger cities, you'll notice that the price board clearly lists two price levels: the cheaper level for the stand-up *bar* and the more expensive for the *tavolo* (table) or *terrazza* (out on the terrace or sidewalk).

Wine:

I would like...	**Vorrei....**	vor-**rehee**
We would like...	**Vorremo...**	vor-**ray**-moh
...a glass	**...un bicchiere**	oon bee-keeay-ray
...a quarter of a liter	**...un quarto litro**	oon **kwar**-toh **lee**-troh
...a half liter	**...un mezzo litro**	oon **mehd**-zoh **lee**-troh
...a carafe	**...una caraffa**	**oo**-nah kah-**rah**-fah
...a half bottle	**...una mezza bottiglia**	**oo**-nah **mehd**-zah boh-**teel**-yah
...a bottle	**...una bottiglia**	**oo**-nah boh-**teel**-yah
...of red wine	**...di rosso**	dee **roh**-soh
...of white wine	**...di bianco**	dee beeahn-koh
...the wine list	**...la lista dei vini**	lah **lee**-stah **dehee vee**-nee

Wine words:

wine / wines	**vino / vini**	**vee**-noh / **vee**-nee
house wine	**vino della casa**	**vee**-noh **dehl**-lah **kah**-zah
local	**locale**	loh-**kah**-lay
red	**rosso**	**roh**-soh
white	**bianco**	beeahn-koh
rosé	**rosato**	roh-**zah**-toh
sparkling	**frizzante**	freet-**sahn**-tay
sweet	**dolce, abboccato**	**dohl**-chay, ah-boh-**kah**-toh
medium	**medio**	**may**-deeoh
dry	**secco**	**say**-koh
very dry	**molto secco**	**mohl**-toh **say**-koh
cork	**tappo**	**tah**-poh

EATING

Italy leads the world in wine production and you'll find it on nearly every table. To save money, order *"Una caraffa di vino della casa"* (a carafe of the house wine). Red wine dominates, as it should. Tuscany is famous for its *chianti*, but also has a good white wine, *Vernaccia*. *Orvieto Classico* is a popular white wine from Umbria. If you like a sweet after-dinner wine, don't miss the *Sciacchetrà* from the *Cinque Terre.* Many small-town Italians in the hotel business have a cellar or cantina which they are proud to show off. They'll often jump at any excuse to descend and drink.

Beer:

beer	**birra**	**bee**-rah
from the tap	**alla spina**	ah-lah **spee**-nah
bottle	**bottiglia**	boh-**teel**-yah
light / dark	**chiara / scura**	keeah-rah / **skoo**-rah
local / imported	**locale / importata**	loh-**kah**-lay / eem-por-**tah**-tah
Italian beer	**birra nazionale**	**bee**-rah naht-seeoh-**nah**-lay
German beer	**birra tedesca**	**bee**-rah tay-**dehs**-kah
Irish beer	**birra irlandese**	**bee**-rah eer-lahn-**day**-zay
small	**piccola**	**pee**-koh-lah
medium	**media**	**may**-deeah
large	**grande**	**grahn**-day
alcohol-free	**analcolica**	ahn-ahl-**koh**-lee-kah
cold	**fredda**	**fray**-dah
colder	**più fredda**	pew **fray**-dah

Bar talk:

What would you like?	**Che cosa prende?**	kay **koh**-zah **prehn**-day
What is the local specialty?	**Qual'è la specialità locale?**	kwah-**leh** lah spay-chah-lee-**tah** loh-**kah**-lay
Straight.	**Liscio.**	**lee**-shoh
With / Without...	**Con / Senza...**	kohn / **sehn**-sah
...alcohol.	**...alcool.**	**ahl**-kohl
...ice.	**...ghiaccio.**	geeah-choh
One more.	**Un altro.**	oon **ahl**-troh
Cheers!	**Cin cin!**	cheen cheen
To your health!	**Salute!**	sah-**loo**-tay
Long life!	**Lunga vita!**	**loong**-gah **vee**-tah
Long live Italy!	**Viva l'Italia!**	**vee**-vah lee-**tahl**-yah
I'm feeling...	**Mi sento...**	mee **sehn**-toh
...a little drunk.	**...un po' ubriaco[a].**	oon poh oo-breeah-koh
...blitzed. (colloq.)	**...ubriaco[a] fradicio[a].**	oo-breeah-koh **frah**-dee-choh

An Italian speciality is *Cinzano,* a red, white, or rosé vermouth. After dinner, try a *digestivo,* a liqueur thought to aid in digestion. For a flammable drink, get *grappa,* firewater distilled from grape skins and stems.

For a memorable and affordable adventure in Venice, have a "pub crawl" dinner. While *cicchetti* (bar munchies) aren't as common as they used to be, many bars (called *ciccheteria*) are still popular for their wide selection of often ugly, always tasty hors d'oeuvres on toothpicks.

EATING

Picnicking

At the market:

Is it self service?	**È self-service?**	eh "self-service"
Ripe for today?	**Per mangiare oggi?**	pehr mahn-**jah**-ray **oh**-jee
Does it need to be cooked?	**Bisogna cucinarlo prima di mangiarlo?**	bee-**zohn**-yah koo-chee-**nar**-loh **pree**-mah dee mahn-**jar**-loh
A little taste?	**Un assaggio?**	oon ah-**sah**-joh
Fifty grams.	**Cinquanta grammi.**	cheeng-**kwahn**-tah **grah**-mee
One hundred grams.	**Un etto.**	oon **eht**-toh
More. / Less.	**Più. / Meno.**	pew / **may**-noh
A piece.	**Un pezzo.**	oon **peht**-soh
A slice.	**Una fettina.**	**oo**-nah fay-**tee**-nah
Sliced.	**Tagliato a fettine.**	tahl-**yah**-toh ah fay-**tee**-nay
A small bag.	**Un sacchettino.**	oon sah-keht-**tee**-noh
A bag, please.	**Un sacchetto, per favore.**	oon sah-**keht**-toh pehr fah-**voh**-ray
Can you make me a sandwich?	**Mi può fare un panino?**	mee pwoh **fah**-ray oon pah-**nee**-noh
To take out.	**Da portar via.**	dah **por**-tar **vee**-ah
Is there a park nearby?	**C'è un parco qui vicino?**	cheh oon **par**-koh kwee vee-**chee**-noh
May we picnic here?	**Va bene fare un picnic qui?**	vah **behn**-nay **fah**-ray oon **peek**-neek kwee
Enjoy your meal!	**Buon appetito!**	bwohn ah-pay-**tee**-toh

Picnic prose:

open air market	**mercato**	mehr-**kah**-toh
grocery store	**alimentari**	ah-lee-mayn-**tah**-ree
supermarket	**supermercato**	soo-pehr-mehr-**kah**-toh
picnic	**picnic**	**peek**-neek
sandwich or roll	**panino**	pah-**nee**-noh
bread	**pane**	**pah**-nay
cured ham (pricey)	**prosciutto crudo**	proh-**shoo**-toh **kroo**-doh
cooked ham	**prosciutto cotto**	proh-**shoo**-toh **kot**-toh
sausage	**salsiccia**	sahl-**see**-chah
cheese	**formaggio**	for-**mah**-joh
mustard...	**senape...**	**say**-nah-pay
mayonnaise..,	**maionese...**	mah-yoh-**nay**-zay
...in a tube	**...in tubetto**	een too-**bay**-toh
yogurt	**yogurt**	**yoh**-goort
fruit	**frutta**	**froo**-tah
box of juice	**cartoccio di succo di frutta**	kar-**toh**-choh dee **soo**-koh dee **froo**-tah
spoon / fork...	**cucchiaio / forchetta...**	koo-keeah-yoh / for-**kay**-tah
...made of plastic	**...di plastica**	dee **plah**-stee-kah
cup / plate...	**bicchiere / piatto,..**	bee-keeay-ray / peeah-toh
...made of paper	**...di carta**	dee **kar**-tah

Make your own sandwiches by getting the ingredients at a market. Order meat and cheese by the gram. One hundred grams (what the Italians call an *etto*) is about a quarter pound, enough for two sandwiches.

Italian-English Menu Decoder

This handy decoder won't list every word on the menu, but it'll help you get *trota* (trout) instead of *trippa* (tripe).

abbocato sweet (wine)
abbacchio lamb (Rome)
acciughe anchovies
aceto vinegar
acqua minerale mineral water
affogato poached
affumicato smoked
aglio garlic
agnello lamb
al dente not overcooked
al forno baked
albicocca apricot
alcool alcohol
all' arrabbiata with bacon, tomato—spicy hot
amatriciana with bacon, tomato, & spices
ananas pineapple
anatra duck
antipasti appetizers
aragosta lobster
arancia orange
aranciata orange soda
aringa herring
arrosto roasted
asparagi asparagus
assortiti assorted
astice male lobster
bacio chocolate hazelnut
barbabietole beets
basilico basil

bevande beverages
bianco white
bibite beverages
bicchiere glass
birra beer
biscotti cookies
bistecca beef steak
bistecca Fiorentina T-bone steak
bollente boiling hot
bollito boiled
bolognese meat & tomato sauce
bottiglia bottle
branzino bass
brioche roll
brodo broth
bruschetta toast with tomatoes
bucatini thick spaghetti
budino pudding
burro butter
caciucco Tuscan fish soup
caffè coffee
calamari squid
caldo hot
calzone folded pizza
cannelloni large tube-shaped noodles
cantucci Tuscan cookies
cappuccino coffee with foam
capra goat
caprese mozzarella & tomato salad

capricciosa chef's specialty
caprino goat cheese
capriolo venison
caraffa carafe
caramelle candy
carbonara with meat sauce
carciofo artichoke
carne meat
carote carrots
carpaccio raw meat
casa house
casalingo homemade
cassata siciliana Sicilian cake
castagne chestnut
cavolfiore cauliflower
cavolo cabbage
cavolini de Bruxelles Brussels sprouts
ceci chickpeas
cena dinner
cervella brains
cervo venison
cetrioli cucumber
cetriolini pickles
cibo food
ciliegia cherry
cinese Chinese
cinghiale boar
cioccolata chocolate
cipolle onions
cocomero watermelon
colazione breakfast
con with
con panna with whipped cream
coniglio rabbit
cono cone
contorni side dishes

coperto cover charge
coppa small bowl
coretto coffee & firewater
cornetto croissant
cotoletta cutlet
cotto cooked
cozze mussels
crèm caramel cream pudding
crema vanilla
crescenza mild cheese
crostata pie with jam
crudo raw
cucina cuisine
cuoco chef
da portar via "to go"
datteri dates
del giorno of the day
della casa of the house
di of
digestivo after-dinner drink
dolce sweet
dolci desserts
dragoncello tarragon
e and
emmenthal Swiss cheese
entrecote sirloin steak
etto one hundred grams
fagiano pheasant
fagioli beans
fagiolini green beans
farcito stuffed
farfalline butterfly-shaped pasta
farinata porridge
fatto in casa homemade
fegato liver
fettina slice
fettucine flat noodles

fico fig
filetto fillet
focaccia flat bread
formaggio cheese
fragola strawberry
frappè milkshake
freddo cold
fresco fresh
frittata omelet
fritto fried
fritto misto fried seafood
frizzante sparkling
frutta fruit
frutti di mare seafood
frutti di bosco berries
funghi mushrooms
gamberetti small shrimp
gamberi shrimp
gamberoni big shrimp
gassata carbonated
gelatina jelly
gelato Italian ice cream
genovese with pesto sauce
ghiaccio ice
giorno day
gnocchi potato noodles
gorgonzola bleu cheese
granchione crab
grande large
granita snow-cone
granturco corn
grappa firewater
griglia grilled
grissini breadsticks
groviera Swiss cheese
gusti flavors
importata imported

incluso included
insalata salad
lampone raspberry
latte milk
latticini small mozzarella balls
lattuga lettuce
leggero light
legumi vegetables
lepre hare
limonata lemon soda
limone lemon
lingua tongue
locale local
maccheroni tube-shaped pasta
macedonia fresh fruit salad
maiale pork
maionese mayonnaise
mandarino tangerine
mandorle almond
manzo beef
margarina margarine
marmellata jam
mascarpone cheese used in desserts
mela apple
melanzana eggplant
melone canteloupe
menta mint
menù turistico fixed-price menu
menù del giorno menu of the day
mercato open air market
merluzzo cod
mezzo half
miele honey
Milanese fried in breadcrumbs
minerale, acqua mineral water
minestra soup

minestrone vegetable soup
mirtillo blueberry
misto mixed
molto very
nero black
nocciola hazelnut
noccioline peanut
noce walnut
noce di cocco coconut
non not
non fumatori non-smoking
o or
olio oil
olive olives
omelette omelet
orata type of fish
ossobuco bone marrow
ostriche oysters
pallina scoop
pancetta thick bacon
pane bread
panforte fruitcake
panino roll, sandwich
panna cream, whipped cream
pansotti pasta stuffed with veggies
parmigiano parmesan cheese
pasticcini pastry
pastina noodles
patate potatoes
patate fritte French fries
penne tube-shaped noodles
pepato with pepper
pepe pepper
peperonata peppers with tomato
  sauce
peperoncino paprika
peperoni bell peppers

pera pear
percorino sheep cheese
pesca peach
pesce fish
pesto basil & olive oil sauce
petto di... breast of...
pezzo piece
piatto plate
piccante spicy hot
piccolo small
piselli peas
pistacchio pistachio
polenta moist cornmeal
pollame poultry
pollo chicken
polpo octopus
pomodori tomatoes
pompelmo grapefruit
pranzo lunch
prezzemolo parsley
prima colazione breakfast
primo piatto first course
prosciutto cured ham
prugna prune
quattro four
ragù meat sauce
ribollita hearty cabbage soup
rigatone tube-shaped noodles
ripieno stuffed
riso rice
risotto saffron-flavored rice
ristorante restaurant
rosato rosé
rosmarino rosemary
rosso red
rosticceria deli
rotelline wheel-shaped pasta

salame pork sausage
salamino piccante pepperoni
salato salty
sale salt
salmone salmon
salsiccia sausage
salvia sage
saporito mild
sarde sardines
scaloppine thin-sliced veal
scampi prawns
secco dry
secondo piatto second course
selvaggina game
senape mustard
senza without
seppia squid
servizio service charge
servizio incluso service included
servizio non incluso service not
  included
sogliola sole
sorbetto sherbet
specialità speciality
spezzatino meat, potato, & tomato
  stew
spinaci spinach
spremuta freshly-squeezed juice
spuntino snack
stagioni seasons (& pizza toppings)
stracchino spreadable cheese
stracciatella chocolate chips with
  vanilla
strapazzate scrambled
stufato stew
succo juice

sugo sauce, usually tomato
susina plum
tacchino turkey
tagliatelle flat noodles
tartina tart
tartufo super-chocolate ice cream
tavola calda fast food
tavolo table
tazza cup
tè tea
tonno tuna
torta cake
torte pie
tortellini stuffed noodles
tovagliolo napkin
tramezzini crustless sandwiches
trippa tripe
trota trout
uova eggs
uva grapes
vegetariano vegetarian
veloce fast
verde green
verdure vegetables
verza cabbage
vino wine
vitello veal
vongole clams
wurstel hot dogs
yogurt yoghurt
zucchero sugar
zuppa soup

Sightseeing

Where is...?	**Dov'è...?**	doh-**veh**
...the best view	**...la vista più bella**	lah **vee**-stah pew **behl**-lah
...the main square	**...la piazza principale**	lah peeaht-sah preen-chee-**pah**-lay
...the old town center	**...il centro storico**	eel **chehn**-troh **stoh**-ree-koh
...the museum	**...il museo**	eel moo-**zay**-oh
...the castle	**...il castello**	eel kah-**stehl**-loh
...the palace	**...il palazzo**	eel pah-**laht**-soh
...the ruins	**...le rovine**	lay roh-**vee**-nay
...tourist information	**...ufficio informazioni**	oo-**fee**-choh een-for-maht-seeoh-nee
...the toilet	**...la toilette**	lah twah-**leht**-tay
...the entrance / exit	**...l'entrata / l'uscita**	lehn-**trah**-tah / loo-**shee**-tah
...a festival	**...un festival**	oon **fehs**-tee-vahl
Do you have...?	**Avete...?**	ah-**vay**-tay
...a map	**...una cartina**	**oo**-nah kar-**tee**-nah
...information	**...informazioni**	een-for-maht-seeoh-nee
...a guidebook	**...una guida**	**oo**-nah **gwee**-dah
...a tour	**...un tour**	oon toor
...in English	**...in inglese**	een een-**glay**-zay
When Is the next tour in English?	**Quando è il prossimo tour in inglese?**	**kwahn**-doh eh eel **pros**-see-moh toor een een-**glay**-zay
Is it free?	**È gratis?**	eh **grah**-tees
How much is it?	**Quanto costa?**	**kwahn**-toh **kos**-tah

Is (the ticket) valid all day?	È valido per tutto il giorno?	eh **vah**-lee-doh pehr **too**-toh eel **jor**-noh
Can I get back in?	Posso rientrare?	**pos**-soh ree-ehn-**trah**-ray
What time does this open / close?	A che ora apre / chiude?	ah kay **oh**-rah **ah**-pray / keeoo-day
What time is the last entry?	Quand'è l'ultima entrata?	kwahn-**deh lool**-tee-mah ayn-**trah**-tah
PLEASE let me in.	PER FAVORE, mi faccia entrare.	pehr fah-**voh**-ray mee **fah**-chah ayn-**trah**-ray
I've traveled all the way from...	Sono venuto[a] qui da...	**soh**-noh vay-**noo**-toh kwee dah
I must leave tomorrow.	Devo partire domani.	**day**-voh par-**tee**-ray doh-**mah**-nee
I promise I'll be fast.	Prometto che sarò veloce.	proh-**may**-toh kay sah-**roh** vay-**loh**-chay

This will help you decipher entrance signs: *adulti* (the price an adult pays), *mostra* (special exhibit), *giro guidato* or *tour* (guided tour), and *siete qui* (means "you are here" on map).

Discounts:

You may be eligible for discounts at tourist sites, hotels, or on buses and trains—ask.

Is there a discount for...?	Fate sconti per...?	fah-tay **skohn**-tee pehr
...youth	...giovani	joh-**vah**-nee
...students	...studenti	stoo-**dehn**-tee
...families	...famiglie	fah-**meel**-yay

...seniors	...anziani	ahn-tseeah-nee
I am...	Sono...	**soh**-noh
He / She is...	Lui / Lei ha...	lwee / **le**hee ah
... ___ years old.	... ___ anni.	ahn-nee

In the museum:

Where is...?	Dov'è...?	doh-**veh**
I'd like to see...	Mi piacerebbe vedere...	mee peeah-chay-**ray**-bay vay-**day**-ray
Photo / video O.K.?	Foto / video è O.K.?	**foh**-toh / **vee**-day-oh eh "O.K."
No flash / tripod.	Vietato usare flash / trepiede.	veeay-**tah**-toh oo-**zah**-ray flahsh / tray-peeay-**day**
I like it.	Mi piace.	mee peeah-chay
It's so...	È così...	eh koh-**zee**
...beautiful.	...bello.	**behl**-loh
...ugly.	...brutto.	**broo**-toh
...strange.	...strano.	**strah**-noh
...boring.	...noioso.	noh-**yoh**-zoh
...interesting.	...interessante.	een-tay-ray-**sahn**-tay
Wow!	Wow!	"wow"
My feet hurt!	Mi fanno male i piedi!	mee **fah**-noh **mah**-lay ee peeay-dee
I'm exhausted!	Sono stanco[a] morto[a]!	**soh**-noh **stahn**-koh **mor**-toh

SIGHTSEEING

Many museums close in the afternoon from 13:00 until 15:00 or 16:00, and are closed all day on a weekday, usually

Monday. Museums often stop selling tickets 45 minutes before closing. Historic churches usually open much earlier than museums.

Art and architecture:

art	**arte**	**ar**-tay
artist	**artista**	ar-**tee**-stah
painting	**quadro**	**kwah**-droh
self portrait	**autoritratto**	ow-toh-ree-**trah**-toh
sculptor	**scultore**	skool-**toh**-ray
sculpture	**scultura**	skool-**too**-rah
architect	**architetto**	ar-kee-**teht**-toh
architecture	**architettura**	ar-kee-teht-**too**-rah
original	**originale**	oh-ree-jee-**nah**-lay
restored	**restaurato**	ray-stow-**rah**-toh
B.C. / A.D.	**A.C. / D.C.**	ah chee / dee chee
century	**secolo**	**say**-koh-loh
style	**stile**	**stee**-lay
Abstract	**Astratto**	ah-**strah**-toh
Ancient	**Antico**	ahn-**tee**-koh
Art Nouveau	**Arte Nouveau**	**ar**-tay **noo**-voh
Baroque	**Barocco**	bah-**rok**-koh
Classical	**Classico**	**klah**-see-koh
Gothic	**Gotico**	**got**-ee-koh
Impressionist	**Impressionista**	eem-pray-seeoh-**nee**-stah
Medieval	**Medievale**	may-deeay-**vah**-lay
Modern	**Moderno**	moh-**dehr**-noh

Neoclassical	**Neoclassico**	nee-oh-**klah**-see-koh
Renaissance	**Rinascimento**	ree-nah-shee-**mayn**-toh
Romanesque	**Romanico**	roh-**mahn**-ee-koh
Romantic	**Romantico**	roh-**mahn**-tee-koh

The Italians refer to their three greatest centuries of art in an unusual way. The 1300s are called *tre cento* (300s). The 1400s (early Renaissance) are called *quattro cento* (400s), and the 1500s (High Renaissance) are *cinque cento* (500s).

Castles and palaces:

castle	**castello**	kah-**stehl**-loh
palace	**palazzo**	pah-**laht**-soh
kitchen	**cucina**	koo-**chee**-nah
cellar	**cantina**	kahn-**tee**-nah
dungeon	**segrete**	say-**gray**-tay
moat	**fossato**	foh-**sah**-toh
fortified walls	**muri fortificati**	**moo**-ree for-tee-fee-**kah**-tee
tower	**torre**	**tor**-ray
fountain	**fontana**	fohn-**tah**-nah
garden	**giardino**	jar-**dee**-noh
king	**re**	ray
queen	**regina**	ray-**jee**-nah
knights	**cavalieri**	kah-vah-lee**ay**-ree

Religious words:

cathedral	**duomo**	**dwoh**-moh
church	**chiesa**	keeay-zah
monastery	**monastero**	moh-nah-**stay**-roh
synagogue	**sinagoga**	see-nah-**gog**-ah
chapel	**cappella**	kah-**pehl**-lah
altar	**altare**	ahl-**tah**-ray
pulpit	**pulpito**	poo-**pee**-toh
cross	**croce**	**kroh**-chay
treasury	**tesoro**	tay-**zoh**-roh
baptistery	**battistero**	bah-tee-**stay**-roh
crypt	**cripta**	**kreep**-tah
dome	**cupola**	**koo**-poh-lah
bells	**campane**	kahm-**pah**-nay
organ	**organo**	**or**-gah-noh
relics	**reliquie**	ray-**lee**-kweeay
saint	**santo[a]**	**sahn**-toh
pope	**Papa**	**pah**-pah
God	**Dio**	**dee**-oh
Jewish	**ebreo**	ay-**bray**-oh
Moslem	**mussulmano[a]**	moo-sool-**mah**-noh
Christian	**cristiano[a]**	kree-steeah-noh
Protestant	**protestante**	proh-tay-**stahn**-tay
Catholic	**cattolico[a]**	kah-**toh**-lee-koh
agnostic	**agnostico[a]**	ahn-**yoh**-stee-koh
atheist	**ateo[a]**	ah-**tay**-oh

| When is the service? | **A che ora è la messa?** | ah kay **oh**-rah eh lah **may**-sah |
| Are there church concerts? | **Ci sono concerti in chiesa?** | chee **soh**-noh kohn-**chehr**-tee een keeay-zah |

The piano was invented in Italy. Unlike a harpsichord, it could be played soft and loud, so it was called just that: *piano-forte* (soft-loud). Here are other Italian musical words you might remember: *subito* (suddenly), *crescendo* (growing louder), *sopra* (over), *sotto* (under), *ritardando* (slowing down), and *fine* (finish).

Shopping

Names of Italian shops:

Where is a...?	**Dov'è un...?**	doh-**veh** oon
antique shop	**negozio di antiquariato**	nay-**goht**-seeoh dee ahn-tee-kwah-reeah-toh
art gallery	**galleria d'arte**	gah-lay-**ree**-ah **dar**-tay
bakery	**panificio**	pah-nee-**fee**-choh
barber shop	**barbiere**	bar-**beeay**-ray
beauty salon	**parrucchiere**	pah-roo-**keeay**-ray
book shop	**libreria**	lee-bray-**ree**-ah
camera shop	**foto-ottica**	foh-toh-**ot**-tee-kah
coffee shop	**barra**	**bah**-rah
department store	**grande magazzino**	**grahn**-day mah-gahd-**zee**-noh

flea market	**mercato delle pulci**	mehr-**kah**-toh **dehl**-lay **pool**-chee
flower market	**mercato dei fiori**	mehr-**kah**-toh **dehee** fee-**oh**-ree
grocery store	**alimentari**	ah-lee-mayn-**tah**-ree
hardware store	**ferramenta**	fehr-rah-**mehn**-tah
jewelry shop	**gioielliera**	joh-yay-lee**ay**-rah
laundromat	**lavanderia**	lah-vahn-day-**ree**-ah
leather shop	**negozio di pelle**	nay-**goht**-seeoh dee **pehl**-lay
newsstand	**giornalaio**	jor-nah-**lah**-yoh
office supplies	**cartoleria**	kar-toh-lay-**ree**-ah
open air market	**mercato**	mehr-**kah**-toh
optician	**ottico**	**ot**-tee-koh
pastry shop	**pasticceria**	pah-stee-chay-**ree**-ah
pharmacy	**farmacia**	far-mah-**chee**-ah
photocopy shop	**copisteria**	koh-pee-stay-**ree**-ah
pottery shop	**negozio di ceramica**	nay-**goht**-seeoh dee chay-**rah**-mee-kah
shopping mall	**centro commerciale**	**chehn**-troh koh-mehr-**chah**-lay
souvenir shop	**negozio di souvenir**	nay-**goht**-seeoh dee **soo**-vay-neer
supermarket	**supermercato**	soo-pehr-mehr-**kah**-toh
toy store	**negozio di giocattoli**	nay-**goht**-seeoh dee joh-**kah**-toh-lee
travel agency	**agenzia di viaggi**	ah-jehnt-**see**-ah dee vee**ah**-jee

used bookstore	**negozio di libri usati**	nay-**goht**-seeoh dee **lee**-bree oo-**zah**-tee
wine shop	**negozio dl vini**	nay-**goht**-seeoh dee **vee**-nee

Most businesses are closed daily from 13:00 until 15:00 or 16:00. Many stores in the larger cities close for all or part of August—not a good time to plan a shopping spree.

Shop till you drop:

opening hours	**orario d'apertura**	oh-**rah**-ree-oh dah-pehr-**too**-rah
sale	**saldo**	**sahl**-doh
How much is it?	**Quanto costa?**	**kwahn**-toh **kos**-tah
I'm / We're...	**Sto / Stiamo...**	stoh / steeah-moh
...just browsing.	**...solo guardando.**	**soh**-loh gwar-**dahn**-doh
Where can I buy...?	**Dove posso comprare...?**	**doh**-vay **pos**-soh kohm-**prah**-ray
I'd like...	**Vorrei...**	vor-**rehee**
Do you have something...?	**Avete qualcosa di...?**	ah-**vay**-tay kwahl-**koh**-zah dee
...cheaper	**...meno caro**	**may**-noh **kah**-roh
...better	**...miglior qualità**	**meel**-yor kwah-lee-**tah**
Can I see more?	**Posso vederne ancora?**	**pos**-soh vay-**dehr**-nay ahn-**koh**-rah
This one.	**Questo qui.**	**kweh**-stoh kwee
Can I try it on?	**Lo posso provare?**	loh **pos**-soh proh-**vah**-ray
Do you have a mirror?	**Ha uno specchio?**	ah **oo**-noh **spay**-keeoh

Too...	Troppo...	trop-poh
...big.	...grande.	grahn-day
...small.	...piccolo.	pee-koh-loh
...expensive.	...caro.	kah-roh
Did you make this?	L'avete fatto voi questo?	lah-vay-tay fah-toh vohee kweh-stoh
What's it made out of?	Di che cosa è fatto?	dee kay koh-zah eh fah-toh
Is it machine washable?	Si può lavare in lavatrice?	see pwoh lah-vah-ray een lah-vah-tree-chay
Will it shrink?	Si ritira?	see ree-tee-rah
Credit card O.K.?	Carta di credito è O.K.?	kar-tah dee kray-dee-toh eh "O.K."
Can you ship this?	Può spedirmelo?	pwoh spay-deer-may-loh
Tax-free?	Esente da tasse?	ay-zehn-tay dah tah-say
I'll think about it.	Ci penserò.	chee pehn-say-roh
What time do you close?	A che ora chiudete?	ah kay oh-rah keeoo-day-tay
What time do you open tomorrow?	A che ora aprite domani?	ah kay oh-rah ah-pree-tay doh-mah-nee
Is that your final price?	È questo il prezzo finale?	eh kweh-stoh eel preht-soh fee-nah-lay
My last offer.	La mia ultima offerta.	lah mee-ah ool-tee-mah oh-fehr-tah
Good price.	Buon prezzo.	bwohn preht-zoh
I'll take it.	La prendo.	lah prehn-doh
I'm nearly broke.	Sono quasi al verde.	soh-noh kwah-zee ahl vehr-day

My male friend...	Il mio amico...	eel **mee**-oh ah-**mee**-koh
My female friend...	La mia amica...	lah **mee**-ah ah-**mee**-kah
My husband...	Mio marito...	**mee**-oh mah-**ree**-toh
My wife...	Mia moglie...	**mee**-ah **mohl**-yay
...has the money.	...ha i soldi.	ah ee **sohl**-dee

You can look up colors and fabrics in the dictionary near the end of this book.

Repair:

These handy lines can apply to any repair, whether it's a stuck zipper, a broken leg, or a dying car.

This is broken.	Questo è rotto.	**kweh**-stoh eh **rot**-toh
Can you fix it?	Lo può aggiustare?	loh pwoh ah-joo-**stah**-ray
Just do the essentials.	Faccia solamente le cose essenziali.	**fah**-chah soh-lah-**mayn**-tay lay **koh**-zay ay-saynt-seeah-lee
How much will it cost?	Quanto costa?	**kwahn**-toh **kos**-tah
When will it be ready?	Quando sarà pronta?	**kwahn**-doh sah-**rah** **pron**-tah
I need it by ___.	Ne ho bisogno entro ___.	nay oh bee-**zohn**-yoh **ayn**-troh

SHOPPING

Entertainment

What's happening tonight?	**Che cosa succede stasera?**	kay **koh**-zah soo-**chay**-day stah-**zay**-rah
What do you recommend?	**Che cosa raccomanda?**	kay **koh**-zah rah-koh-**mahn**-dah
Is it free?	**È gratis?**	eh **grah**-tees
Where can I buy a ticket?	**Dove si comprano i biglietti?**	**doh**-vay see kohm-**prah**-noh ee beel-**yay**-tee
When does it start?	**A che ora comincia?**	ah kay **oh**-rah koh-**meen**-chah
When does it end?	**A che ora finisce?**	ah kay **oh**-rah fee-**nee**-shay
Will you go out with me?	**Vuole uscire con me?**	**vwoh**-lay oo-**shee**-ray kohn may
Where's the best place to dance nearby?	**Qual'è il posto migliore per ballare qui vicino?**	kwah-**leh** eel **poh**-stoh meel-**yoh**-ray pehr bah-**lah**-ray kwee vee-**chee**-noh
Do you want to dance?	**Vuoi ballare?**	**vwoh**ee bah-**lah**-ray
Let's have a wild and crazy night!	**Diamoci una notte da sballo!**	deeah-**moh**-chee **oo**-nah **not**-tay dah **zbah**-loh
Where do people stroll?	**Dov'è la passeggiata?**	doh-**veh** lah pah-say-**jah**-tah

For cheap entertainment, join the locals and take a *passeggiata* (stroll) through town. As you bump shoulders in the crowd, you'll know why it's also called *struscio* (rubbing). On workdays, Italians stroll between work and dinner. On holidays, they hit the streets after lunch. This is Italy on parade. People are strutting. If ever you could enjoy being forward, this is the time. Whispering a breathy *bella* (cute girl) or *bello* (cute guy) feels natural.

Entertaining words:

movie...	**cinema...**	**chee**-nay-mah
...original version	**...versione originale**	vehr-see**oh**-nay oh-ree-jee-**nah** lay
...in English	**...in inglese**	een een-**glay**-zay
...with subtitles	**...con sottotitoli**	kohn soh-toh-**tee**-toh-lee
...dubbed	**...doppiato**	doh-pee**ah**-toh
music...	**musica...**	**moo**-zee-kah
...live	**...dal vivo**	dahl **vee**-voh
...classical	**...classica**	**klah**-see-kah
...folk	**...folk**	fohlk
old rock	**rock vecchio stile**	rok **vehk**-eeoh **stee**-lay
jazz / blues	**jazz / blues**	jahzz / "blues"
singer	**cantante**	kahn-**tahn**-tay
concert	**concerto**	kohn-**chehr**-toh
show	**spettacolo**	spay-**tah**-koh-loh
dancing	**ballare**	bah-**lah**-ray
folk dancing	**danze popolari**	**dahnt**-say poh-poh-**lah**-ree
disco	**discoteca**	dee-skoh-**tay**-kah
no cover charge	**ingresso libero**	een-**gray**-soh **lee**-bay-roh

ENTERTAINMENT

Phoning

Where is the nearest phone?	**Dov'è il telefono più vicino?**	doh-**veh** eel tay-**lay**-foh-noh pew vee-**chee**-noh
I'd like to telephone...	**Vorrei fare una telefonata...**	vor-**rehee** fah-ray **oo**-nah tay-lay-foh-**nah**-tah
...the United States.	**...negli Stati Uniti.**	**nayl**-yee **stah**-tee oo-**nee**-tee
How much per minute?	**Quanto costa al minuto?**	**kwahn**-toh **kos**-tah ahl mee-**noo**-toh
I'd like to make a... call.	**Vorrei fare una telefonata...**	vor-**rehee** fah-ray **oo**-nah tay-lay-foh-**nah**-tah
...local	**...urbana.**	oor-**bah**-nah
...collect	**...a carico del destinatario.**	ah **kah**-ree-koh dayl dehs-tee-nah-**tah**-reeoh
...credit card	**...con la carta di credito.**	kohn lah **kar**-tah dee **kray**-dee-toh
...long distance (within Italy)	**...interurbana.**	een-tay-roor-**bah**-nah
...international	**...internazionale.**	een-tehr-naht-seeoh-**nah**-lay
It doesn't work.	**Non funziona.**	nohn foont-seeoh-nah
May I use your phone?	**Posso usare il telefono?**	**pos**-soh oo-**zah**-ray eel tay-**lay**-foh-noh
Can you dial for me?	**Può fare il numero per me?**	pwoh **fah**-ray eel **noo**-may-roh pehr may
Can you talk for me?	**Può parlare per me?**	pwoh par-**lah**-ray pehr may
It's busy.	**È occupato.**	eh oh-koo-**pah**-toh
Will you try again?	**Può riprovare?**	pwoh ree-proh-**vah**-ray

Hello. (answering the phone)	**Pronto.**	**pron**-toh
My name is...	**Mi chiamo...**	mee keeah-moh
My number is...	**Il mio numero è...**	eel mee-oh **noo**-may-roh eh
Speak slowly and clearly.	**Parli lentamente e chiaramente.**	**par**-lee layn-tah-**mayn**-tay ay keeah-rah-**mayn**-tay
Wait a moment.	**Un momento.**	oon moh-**mayn**-toh
Don't hang up.	**Non agganci.**	nohn ah-**gahn**-chee

Key telephone words:

telephone	**telefono**	tay-**lay**-foh-noh
telephone card	**carta telefonica**	**kar**-tah tay-lay-**foh**-nee-kah
operator	**centralinista**	chayn-trah-lee-**nee**-stah
international assistance	**assistenza per chiamate internazionali**	ah-see-**stehnt**-sah pehr keeah-**mah**-tay een-tehr-naht-seeoh-**nah**-lee
country code	**prefisso per il paese**	pray-**fee**-soh pehr eel pah-**ay**-zay
area code	**prefisso**	pray-**fee**-soh
telephone book	**elenco telefonico**	ay-**lehn**-koh tay-lay-**foh**-nee-koh
yellow pages	**pagine gialle**	**pah**-jee-nay **jah**-lay
metered phone	**telefono a scatti**	tay-**lay**-foh-noh ah **skah**-tee
phone booth	**cabina telefonica**	kah-**bee**-nah tay-lay-**foh**-nee-kah
place to make public phone calls	**posto telefonico pubblico**	**pos**-toh tay-lay-**foh**-nee-koh **poo**-blee-koh

PHONING, E-MAIL

| out of service | **guasto** | gooah-stoh |

When dealing on the phone with someone who only speaks Italian, you might try asking someone to talk for you on your end.

The public phones use coins or a telephone card (*carta telefonica*). These easy-to-use phone cards are sold at post offices, train stations, *tabacchi* (tobacco shops), and machines near phone booths. Tear the corner off your phone card before using it.

You can call locally or internationally from public phone booths, post offices, and metered phones in cafés and bars. If you get a wrong number, you'll hear the dreaded recording: *"Il numero da Lei composte è inesistente."* For more information, see "Let's Talk Telephones."

E-mail

e-mail	**posta elettronica**	**pos**-tah ay-leht-**troh**-nee-kah
internet	**internet**	een-tehr-neht
May I check my e-mail?	**Posso controllare la posta elettronica?**	**pos**-soh kohn-troh-**lah**-ray lah **pos**-tah ay-leht-**troh**-nee-kah
Where can I get access to the internet?	**C'è un posto dove posso accedere a internet?**	cheh oon **pos**-toh **doh**-vay **pos**-soh ah-**chay**-day-ray ah **een**-tehr-neht
Where is the nearest cybercafé?	**Dov'è il caffè cibernetico più vicino?**	doh-**veh** eel kah-**feh** chee-behr-**nay**-tee-koh pew vee-**chee**-noh

On the computer screen:

aprire	open	**messaggio**	message
cancellare	delete	**salvare**	save
documento	file	**stampare**	print
inviare	send		

Post Office

Where is the post office?	**Dov'è la Posta?**	dòh-**veh** lah **poh**-stah
Which window for...?	**Qual'è lo sportello per...?**	kwah-**leh** loh spor-**tehl**-loh pehr
Is this the line for...?	**È questa la fila per...?**	eh **kweh**-stah lah **fee**-lah pehr
...stamps	**...francobolli**	frahn-koh-**boh**-lee
...packages	**...pacchi**	**pah**-kee
To the United States...	**Per Stati Uniti...**	pehr **stah**-tee oo-**nee**-tee
...by air mail.	**...per via aerea.**	pehr **vee**-ah ah-**ay**-ray-ah
...slow and cheap.	**...lento e economico.**	**lehn**-toh ay ay-koh-**noh**-mee-koh
How much is it?	**Quanto costa?**	**kwahn**-toh **kos**-tah
How many days will it take?	**Quanti giorni ci vogliono?**	**kwahn**-tee **jor**-nee chee **vohl**-yoh-noh

Licking the postal code:

Post & Telegraph Office	**Poste e Telegrafi**	**poh**-stah ay tay-**lay**-grah-fee
post office	**ufficio postale**	oo-**fee**-choh poh-**stah**-lay
stamp	**francobollo**	frahn-koh-**boh**-loh
postcard	**cartolina**	kar-toh-**lee**-nah
letter	**lettera**	**leht**-tay-rah
aerogram	**aerogramma**	ah-ay-roh-**grah**-mah
envelope	**busta**	**boo**-stah
package	**pacco**	**pah**-koh
box...	**scatola...**	**skah**-toh-lah
...cardboard	**...de cartone**	day kar-**toh**-nay
string / tape	**filo / scotch**	**fee**-loh / "scotch"
mailbox	**cassetta postale**	kah-**say**-tah poh-**stah**-lay
air mail	**per via aerea**	pehr **vee**-ah ah-**ay**-ray-ah
express	**espresso**	ay-**sprehs**-soh
slow and cheap	**lento e economico**	**lehn**-toh ay ay-koh-**noh**-mee-koh
book rate	**prezzo di listino**	**preht**-soh dee lee-**stee**-noh
weight limit	**limite di peso**	lee-**mee**-tay dee **pay**-zoh
registered	**raccomandata**	rah-koh-mahn-**dah**-tah
insured	**assicurato**	ah-see-koo-**rah**-toh
fragile	**fragile**	frah-**jee**-lay
contents	**contenuto**	kohn-tay-**noo**-toh
customs	**dogana**	doh-**gah**-nah
sender	**mittente**	mee-**tehn**-tay
destination	**destinatario**	dehs-tee-nah-**tah**-reeoh

to / from	**da / a**	dah / ah
address	**indirizzo**	een-dee-**reet**-soh
zip code	**codice postale**	koh-**dee**-chay poh-**stah**-lay
general delivery	**fermo posta**	**fehr**-moh **poh**-stah

In Italy, you can often get stamps at the corner *tabacchi* (tobacco shop). As long as you know which stamps you need, this is a great convenience. Unless you like to gamble, avoid mailing packages from Italy. The most reliable post offices are in the Vatican City.

Red Tape & Profanity

Filling out Italian forms:

Signore / Signora / Signorina	Mr. / Mrs. / Miss
nome	first name
cognome	name
indirizzo	address
domicilio	address
strada	street
città	city
stato	state
paese	country
nazionalità	nationality
origine / destinazione	origin / destination
età	age
data di nascita	date of birth
luogo di nascita	place of birth
sesso	sex
sposato / sposata	married man / married woman
scapolo / nubile	single man / single woman
professione	profession
adulto	adult
bambino / ragazzo / ragazza	child / boy / girl
bambini	children
famiglia	family
firma	signature

When filling out dates, use this order: day/month/year (Christmas is 25/12/01).

Italian profanity:

In any country, red tape inspires profanity. In case you're wondering what the more colorful locals are saying...

Damn it.	Dannazione.	dah-naht-see**oh**-nay
Screw it.	Vai a fa'n culo.	**vah**ee ah fahn **koo**-loh
Stick it between	Ficcatelo	fee-kah-**tay**-loh
your teeth.	tra i denti.	trah ee **dayn**-tee
Go to hell.	Vai al diavolo.	**vah**ee ahl dee**ah**-voh-loh
bastard	bastardo	bah-**star**-doh
bitch	cagna	**kahn**-yah
breasts (colloq.)	pocce	**poch**-ay
penis (colloq.)	cazzo	**kaht**-soh
butthole	stronzo	**stront**-soh
shit	merda	**mehr**-dah
drunk	ubriaco	oo-bree**ah**-koh
idiot	idiota	ee-dee**oh**-tah
jerk	imbecille	eem-bay-**chee**-lay
stupid	stupido	**stoo**-pee-doh
Did someone fart?	Ma qualcuno	mah kwahl-**koo**-noh
	ha fatto una	ah **fah**-toh **oo**-nah
	scoreggia?	skoh-**ray**-jah
I burped.	Ho ruttato.	oh roo-**tah**-toh

Help!

Help!	**Aiuto!**	ah-**yoo**-toh
Help me!	**Aiutatemi!**	ah-yoo-**tah**-tay-mee
Call a doctor!	**Chiamate un dottore!**	keeah-**mah**-tay oon doh-**toh**-ray
ambulance	**ambulanza**	ahm-boo-**lahnt**-sah
accident	**incidente**	een-chee-**dehn**-tay
injured	**ferito**	fay-**ree**-toh
emergency	**emergenza**	ay-mehr-**jehnt**-sah
emergency room	**pronto soccorso**	**pron**-toh soh-**kor**-soh
fire	**fuoco**	**fwoh**-koh
police	**polizia**	poh-leet-**see**-ah
thief	**ladro**	**lah**-droh
pick-pocket	**borsaiolo**	bor-sah-**yoh**-loh
I've been ripped off.	**Sono stato[a] imbrogliato[a].**	**soh**-noh **stah**-toh eem-brohl-**yah**-toh
I've lost my...	**Ho perso il mio...**	oh **pehr**-soh eel **mee**-oh
...passport.	**...passaporto.**	pah-sah-**por**-toh
...ticket.	**...biglietto.**	beel-**yay**-toh
...baggage.	**...bagaglio.**	bah-**gahl**-yoh
...wallet.	**...portafoglio.**	por-tah-**fohl**-yoh
I've lost...	**Ho perso...**	oh **pehr**-soh
...my purse.	**...la mia borsa.**	la **mee**-ah **bor**-sah
...my faith in humankind.	**...la fiducia nel prossimo.**	lah fee-**doo**-chah nayl **pros**-see-moh
I'm lost.	**Mi sono perso[a].**	mee **soh**-noh **pehr**-soh

In Italy, call 118 if you have a medical emergency.

Help for women:

English	Italian	Pronunciation
Leave me alone.	**Mi lasci in pace.**	mee **lah**-shee een **pah**-chay
I *vant* to be alone.	**Voglio stare sola.**	**vohl**-yoh **stah**-ray **soh**-lah
I'm not interested.	**Non sono interessata.**	nohn **soh**-noh een-tay-ray-**sah**-tah
I'm married.	**Sono sposata.**	**soh**-noh spoh **zah**-tah
I'm a lesbian.	**Sono lesbica.**	**soh**-noh **lehz**-bee-kah
I have a contagious disease.	**Ho una malattia contagiosa.**	oh **oo**-nah mah-lah-**tee**-ah kohn-tah-**joh**-zah
You are intrusive.	**Mi sta dando fastidio.**	mee stah **dahn**-doh fah-**stee**-deeoh
This man is bothering me.	**Questo uomo mi importuna.**	**kweh**-stoh **woh**-moh mee eem-por-**too**-nah
Don't touch me.	**Non mi tocchi.**	nohn mee **toh**-kee
You're disgusting.	**Tu sei disgustoso.**	too **seh**ee dees-goo-**stoh**-zoh
Stop following me.	**La smetta di seguirmi.**	lah **zmay**-tah dee **say**-gweer-mee
Enough!	**Basta!**	**bah**-stah
Go away.	**Se ne vada.**	say nay **vah**-dah
Get lost!	**Sparisca!**	spah-**ree**-skah
Drop dead!	**Crepi!**	**kray**-pee
I'll call the police.	**Chiamo la polizia.**	keeah-moh lah poh-leet-**see**-ah

Whenever macho males threaten to make leering a contact sport, local women stroll arm-in-arm or holding hands. Wearing conservative clothes and avoiding smiley eye contact also convey a "don't hustle me" message.

Health

I feel sick.	**Mi sento male.**	mee **sehn**-toh **mah**-lay
I need a doctor...	**Ho bisogno di un dottore...**	oh bee-**zohn**-yoh dee oon doh-**toh**-ray
...who speaks English.	**...che parli inglese.**	kay **par**-lee een-**glay**-zay
It hurts here.	**Fa male qui.**	fah **mah**-lay kwee
I'm allergic to...	**Sono allergico[a]...**	**soh**-noh ah-**lehr**-jee-koh
...penicillin.	**...alla penicillina.**	**ah**-lah pay-nee-chee-**lee**-nah
I am diabetic.	**Ho il diabete.**	oh eel deeah-**bay**-tay
I've missed a period.	**Ho saltato il ciclo mestruale.**	oh sahl-**tah**-toh eel **chee**-kloh may-stroo-**ah**-lay
My male friend has...	**Il mio amico ha...**	eel **mee**-oh ah-**mee**-koh ah
My female friend has...	**La mia amica ha...**	lah **mee**-ah ah-**mee**-kah ah
I have...	**Ho...**	oh
...asthma.	**...l'asma.**	**lahz**-mah
...athelete's foot.	**...mal di piedi.**	mahl dee peeay-dee
...bug bites.	**...morsicatura d'insetto.**	mor-see-kah-**too**-rah deen-**seht**-toh
...a burn.	**...un bruciatura.**	oon broo-chah-**too**-rah
...chest pains.	**...dolore al petto.**	doh-**loh**-ray ahl **peht**-toh
...a cold.	**...un raffreddore.**	oon rah-fray-**doh**-ray
...constipation.	**...stitichezza.**	stee-tee-**kayt**-sah
...a cough.	**...la tosse.**	lah **tos**-say
...diarrhea.	**...diarrea.**	dee-ah-**ray**-ah
...dizziness.	**...la testa che gira.**	lah **tehs**-tah kay **jee**-rah
...a fever.	**...la febbre.**	lah **fehb**-bray
...hemorrhoids.	**...le emorroidi.**	lay ay-moh-roh**ee**-dee

...the flu.	...l'influenza.	leen-floo-**ehnt**-sah
...the giggles.	...la ridarella.	lah ree-dah-**ray**-lah
...hay fever.	...il raffreddore da fieno.	eel rah-fray-**doh**-ray dah feeay-noh
...a headache.	...un mal di testa.	oon mahl dee **tehs**-tah
...high blood pressure.	...la pressione alta.	lah pray-seeoh-nay **ahl**-tah
...indigestion.	...una indigestione.	**oo**-nah een-dee-jay-steeoh-nay
...an infection.	...una infezione.	**oo**-nah een-fay-tseeoh-nay
...a migraine.	...l'emicrania.	lay-mee-**krah**-nee-ah
...nausea.	...nausea.	**now**-zee-ah
...a rash.	...una infiammazione.	**oo**-nah een-feeah-maht-seeoh-nay
...a sore throat.	...la gola infiammata.	lah **goh**-lah een-feeah-**mah**-tah
...a stomach ache.	...il mal di stomaco.	eel mahl dee **stom**-ah-koh
...swelling.	...un gonfiore.	oon gohn-feeoh-ray
...a toothache.	...mal di denti.	mahl dee **dehn**-tee
...a venereal disease.	...una malattia venerea.	**oo**-nah mah-lah-**tee**-ah vay-nay-**ray**-ah
...urinary infection.	...infezione urinaria.	een-feht-seeoh-nay oo-ree-**nah**-reeah
...worms.	...vermi.	**vehr**-mee
I have body odor.	Puzzo.	**poot**-soh
Is it serious?	È grave?	eh **grah**-vay

Handy health words:

pain	**dolore**	doh-**loh**-ray
dentist	**dentista**	dayn-**tee**-stah
doctor	**dottore**	doh-**toh**-ray
nurse	**infermiera**	een-fehr-mee**ay**-rah
health insurance	**assicurazione medica**	ah-see-koo-raht-see**oh**-nay **mehd**-ee-kah
hospital	**ospedale**	oh-spay-**dah**-lay
blood	**sangue**	**sahn**-gway
bandage	**cerotti**	chay-**rot**-tee
medicine	**medicina**	may-dee-**chee**-nah
pharmacy	**farmacia**	far-mah-**chee**-ah
prescription	**prescrizione**	pray-skreet-see**oh**-nay
pill	**pillola**	**pee**-loh-lah
aspirin	**aspirina**	ah-spee-**ree**-nah
non-aspirin substitute	**Saridon**	**sah**-ree-dohn
antibiotic	**antibiotici**	ahn-tee-bee**oh**-tee-chee
cold medicine	**medicina per il raffreddore**	may-dee-**chee**-nah pehr eel rah-fray-**doh**-ray
cough drops	**sciroppo per la tosse**	skee-**roh**-poh pehr lah **tos**-say
antacid	**antiacido**	ahn-teeah-**chee**-doh
pain killer	**analgesico**	ah-nahl-**jehz**-ee-koh
Preparation H	**Preparazione H**	pray-pah-raht-see**oh**-nay **ah**-kah
vitamins	**vitamine**	vee-tah-**mee**-nay

Contacts and glasses:

glasses	occhiali	oh-keeah-lee
sunglasses	occhiali da sole	oh-keeah-lee dah soh-lay
prescription	ricetta	ree-cheh-tah
lenses...	lenti...	lehn-tee
...soft / hard	...morbide / dure	mor-bee-day / doo-ray
disposable lens	lenti usa e getta	lehn-tee oo-zah ay jeh-tah
cleaning solution	soluzione al sapone	soh-loot-seeoh-nay ahl sah-poh-nay
soaking solution	solvente	cohl vehn-lay
I've... a contact lens.	Ho... una lente a contatto.	oh... oo-nah lehn-tay ah kohn-tah-toh
...lost	...perso	pehr-soh
...swallowed	...inghiottito	een-goht-tee-toh

Toiletries:

comb	pettine	pay-tee-nay
conditioner	balsamo	bahl-sah-moh
condoms	preservativi	pray-zehr-vah-tee-vee
dental floss	filo interdentale	fee-loh een-tehr-dayn-tah-lay
deodorant	deodorante	day-oh-doh-rahn-tay
hairbrush	spazzola per capelli	spaht-soh-lah pehr kah-pehl-lee
hand lotion	crema per le mani	kray-mah pehr lay mah-nee
lip salve	burro di cacao	boor-roh dee kah-kah-oh
nail clipper	tagliaunghie	tahl-yah-oong-geeay

HEALTH

razor	**rasoio**	rah-**zoh**-yoh
sanitary napkins	**assorbenti igienici**	ah-sor-**bayn**-tee ee-jay-**nee**-chee
shampoo	**shampoo**	**shahm**-poh
shaving cream	**crema da barba**	**kray**-mah dah **bar**-bah
soap	**sapone**	sah-**poh**-nay
sunscreen	**protezione solare**	proh-tayt-see**oh**-nay soh-**lah**-ray
tampons	**assorbenti interni**	ah-sor-**bayn**-tee een-**tehr**-nee
tissues	**fazzoletti di carta**	faht-soh-**leht**-tee dee **kar**-tah
toilet paper	**carta igienica**	**kar**-tah ee-**jay**-nee-kah
toothbrush	**spazzolino da denti**	spaht-soh-**lee**-noh dah **dayn**-tee
toothpaste	**dentifricio**	dayn-tee-**free**-choh
tweezers	**pinzette**	peent-**say**-tay

Chatting

My name is...	**Mi chiamo...**	mee keeah-moh
What's your name?	**Come si chiama?**	**koh**-may see keeah-mah
This is...	**Le presento...**	lay pray-**zehn**-toh
How are you?	**Come sta?**	**koh**-may stah
Very well, thank you.	**Molto bene,**	**mohl**-toh **behn**-ay
	grazie.	**graht**-seeay
Where are you from?	**Di dove è?**	dee **doh**-vay eh
What... are you from?	**Da che... viene?**	dah kay... vee**ay**-nay
...city	**...città**	choo-**tah**
...country	**...paese**	pah-**ay**-zay
...planet	**...pianeta**	peeah-**nay**-tah
I'm...	**Sono...**	**soh**-noh
...American.	**...Americano[a].**	ah-may-ree-**kah**-noh
...Canadian.	**...Canadese.**	kah-nah-**day**-zay

Nothing more than feelings:

I am / You are...	**Sono / È...**	**soh**-noh / eh
...happy.	**...felice.**	fay-**lee**-chay
...sad.	**...triste.**	**tree**-stay
...tired.	**...stanco[a].**	**stahn**-koh
...lucky.	**...fortunato[a].**	for-too-**nah**-toh
I am / You are...	**Ho / Ha...**	oh / ah
...hungry / thirsty.	**...fame / sete.**	**fah**-may / **say**-tay
...homesick.	**...nostalgia.**	noh-**stahl**-jah
...cold.	**...freddo.**	**fray**-doh
...too warm.	**...troppo caldo.**	**trop**-poh **kahl**-doh

CHATTING

Who's who:

My...	Mio / Mia...	**mee**-oh / **mee**-ah
...male friend / female friend.	...amico / amica.	ah-**mee**-koh / ah-**mee**-kah
...boyfriend / girlfriend.	...ragazzo / ragazza.	rah-**gaht**-soh / rah-**gaht**-sah
...husband / wife.	...marito / moglie.	mah-**ree**-toh / **mohl**-yay
...son / daughter.	...figlio / figlia.	**feel**-yoh / **feel**-yah
...brother / sister.	...fratello / sorella.	frah-**tehl**-loh / soh-**rehl**-lah
...father / mother.	...padre / madre.	**pah**-dray / **mah**-dray
...uncle / aunt.	...zio / zia.	**tsee**oh / **tsee**ah
...nephew or niece.	...nipote.	nee-**poh**-tay
...male / female cousin.	...cugino / cugina.	koo-**gee**-noh / koo-**gee**-nah
...grandfather / grandmother.	...nonno / nonna.	**noh**-noh / **noh**-nah
...grandchild.	...nipote.	nee-**poh**-tay

Family and work:

Are you married? (asked of a woman)	È sposata?	eh spoh-**zah**-tah
Are you married? (asked of a man)	È sposato?	eh spoh-**zah**-toh
Do you have children?	Ha bambini?	ah bahm-**bee**-nee
How many boys and girls?	Quanti ragazzi e ragazze?	**kwahn**-tee rah-**gaht**-zee ay rah-**gaht**-zay
Do you have photos?	Ha foto?	ah **foh**-toh
How old is your child?	Quanti anni ha il suo bambino?	**kwahn**-tee **ahn**-nee ah eel **soo**-oh bahm-**bee**-noh

Beautiful child!	**Bel bambino!**	behl bahm-**bee**-noh
Beautiful children!	**Bei bambini!**	**beh**ee bahm-**bee**-nee
What is your job?	**Che lavoro fa?**	kay lah-**voh**-roh fah
Do you like your work?	**Le piace il suo lavoro?**	lay peeah-chay eel **soo**-oh lah-**voh**-roh
I'm a...	**Sono...**	**soh**-noh
...male student / female student.	**...studente / studentessa.**	stoo-**dehn**-tay / stoo-dehn-**tehs**-sah
...teacher.	**...insegnante.**	een-sayn-**yahn**-tay
...worker.	**...operaio[a].**	oh-pay-**rah**-yoh
...bureaucrat.	**...burocrate.**	boo-roh-**kray**-tay
...brain surgeon.	**...chirurgo del cervello.**	kee-**roor**-goh dayl chehr-**vehl**-loh
...professional traveler.	**...turista di professione.**	too-**ree**-stah dee proh-fay-**seeoh**-nay
Can I take a photo of you?	**Posso far le uno fotografia?**	**pos**-soh **far** lay **oo**-noh foh-toh-grah-**fee**-ah

Chatting with children:

What's your name?	**Come ti chiami?**	**koh**-may tee keeah-mee
My name is...	**Mi chiamo...**	mee keeah-moh
How old are you?	**Quanti anni hai?**	**kwahn**-tee **ahn**-nee ahee
Do you have brothers and sisters?	**Hai fratelli e sorelle?**	ahee frah-**tehl**-lee ay soh-**rehl**-lay
Do you like school?	**Ti piace la scuola?**	tee peeah-chay lah skoo-**oh**-lah

What are you studying?	**Che cosa stai studiando?**	kay **koh**-zah **stah**ee stoo-deeahn-doh
I'm studying...	**Sto studiando...**	stoh stoo-deeahn-doh
What's your favorite subject?	**Qual'è la tua materia favorita?**	kwah-leh lah **too**-ah mah-tay-ree-ah fah-voh-**ree**-tah
Do you have pets?	**Hai animali domestici?**	ahee ah-nee-**mah**-lee doh-mehs-**tee**-chee
...cat / dog / fish	**...gatto / cane / pesce**	**gah**-toh / **kah**-nay / **peh**-shay
I have a...	**Ho un...**	oh oon
Will you teach me some Italian words?	**Mi insegni delle parole in italiano?**	mee een-**sayn**-yee **dehl**-lay pah-**roh**-lay een ee-tah-leeah-noh
What is this?	**Che cos'è?**	kay **koh**-zeh
Will you teach me a simple Italian song?	**Mi insegni una canzone italiana facile?**	mee een-**sayn**-yee **oo**-nah kahnt-**soh**-nay ee-tah-leeah-nah fah-**chee**-lay
Guess which country I live in.	**Indovina in quale paese vivo.**	een-doh-**vee**-nah een **kwah**-lay pah-**ay**-zay **vee**-voh
How old am I?	**Quanti anni ho?**	**kwahn**-tee **ahn**-nee oh
I'm ___ years old.	**Ho ___ anni.**	oh ___ **ahn**-nee
Want to thumb-wrestle?	**Vuoi fare la lotta con i pollici?**	vwohee **fah**-ray lah **lot**-tah kohn ee pol-**lee**-chee
Want to hear me burp?	**Mi vuoi sentire ruttare?**	mee **vwoh**ee sehn-**tee**-ray roo-**tah**-ray
Teach me a fun game.	**Mi insegni un gioco divertente.**	mee een-**sayn**-yee oon **joh**-koh dee-vehr-**tehn**-tay
Got any candy?	**Hai una caramella?**	ahee **oo**-nah kah-rah-**mehl**-lah

Favorite things:

What... do you like?	**Qual'è Il suo... preferito?**	kwah-**leh** eel **soo**-oh... pray-fay-**ree**-toh
...art	**...genere d'arte**	**jay**-nay-ray **dar**-tay
...books	**...genere di libri**	**jay**-nay-ray dee **lee**-bree
...hobby	**...passatempo**	pah-sah-**tehm**-poh
...ice cream	**...gelato**	jay-**lah**-toh
...movie	**...film**	feelm
...male movie star	**...attore**	ah-**toh**-ray
...music	**...genere di musica**	**jay**-nay-ray dee **moo**-zee-kah
...male singer	**...cantante**	kahn-**tahn**-tay
...sport	**...sport**	sport
...vice	**...vizio**	**veet**-seeoh
What... do you like?	**Qual'è la sua... preferita?**	kwah-**leh** lah **soo**-ah... pray-fay-**ree**-tah
...female movie star	**...attrice**	ah-**tree**-chay
...female singer	**...cantante**	kahn-**tahn**-tay

Responses for all occasions:

I like that.	**Mi piace.**	mee pee**ah**-chay
I like you.	**Lei mi piace.**	**le**hee mee pee**ah**-chay
Great!	**Ottimo!**	**ot**-tee-moh
What a nice place.	**Che bel posto.**	kay behl **pos**-toh
Perfect.	**Perfetto.**	pehr-**feht**-toh
Funny.	**Divertente.**	dee-vehr-**tehn**-tay
Interesting.	**Interessante.**	een-tay-ray-**sahn**-tay

CHATTING

I don't smoke.	**Non fumo.**	nohn **foo**-moh
I haven't any.	**Non ne ho.**	nohn nay oh
Really?	**Davvero?**	dah-**vay**-roh
Congratulations!	**Congratulazioni!**	kohn-grah-too-laht-see**oh**-nee
Well done!	**Bravo[a]!**	**brah**-voh
You're welcome.	**Prego.**	**pray**-goh
Bless you!	**Salute!**	sah-**loo**-tay
(after sneeze)		
Excuse me.	**Mi scusi.**	mee **skoo**-zee
What a pity.	**Che peccato.**	kay pehk-**kah**-toh
That's life.	**È così.**	eh koh-**zee**
No problem.	**Non c'è problema.**	nohn cheh proh-**blay**-mah
O.K.	**Va bene.**	vah **behn**-ay
I feel like a pope!	**Sto come un papa!**	stoh **koh**-may oon **pah**-pah
(happy)		
This is the good life!	**Questa sì che è vita!**	**kweh**-stah see kay eh **vee**-tah
Have a good day!	**Buona giornata!**	**bwoh**-nah jor-**nah**-tah
Good luck!	**Buona fortuna!**	**bwoh**-nah for-**too**-nah
Let's go!	**Andiamo!**	ahn-dee**ah**-moh

Thanks a million:

A thousand thanks.	**Grazie mille.**	**graht**-seeay **mee**-lay
You are...	**Lei è...**	**le**hee eh
...kind.	**...gentile.**	jayn-**tee**-lay
...helpful.	**...di aiuto.**	dee ah-**yoo**-toh
...generous.	**...generoso[a].**	jay-nay-**roh**-zoh

It's / You are...	È / Lei è...	eh / **leh**ee eh
...great.	...ottimo.	**ot**-tee-moh
...great fun.	...un vero divertimento.	oon **vay**-roh dee-vehr-tee-**mayn**-toh
You've gone to much trouble.	Si è veramente disturbato[a].	see eh vay-rah-**mayn**-tay dee-stoor-**bah**-toh
You are a saint.	Lei è un santo[a].	**leh**ee eh oon **sahn**-toh
You spoil me / us.	Mi (Ci) viziate.	mee (chee) veet-**see**ah-tay
I will remember you...	Mi ricorderò di Lei...	mee ree-kor-day-**roh** dee **leh**ee
...always.	...sempre.	**sehm**-pray
...till Tuesday.	...fino a martedì.	**fee**-noh ah mar-tay-**dee**

Travel talk:

I am / Are you...?	Sono / È...?	**soh**-noh / eh
...on vacation	...In vacanza	een vah-**kahnt**-sah
...on business	...qui per lavoro	kwee pehr lah-**voh**-roh
How long have you been traveling?	Da quanto tempo è in viaggio?	dah **kwahn**-toh **tehm**-poh eh een vee**ah**-joh
day / week	giorno / settimana	**jor**-noh / say-tee-**mah**-nah
month / year	mese / anno	**may**-zay / **ahn**-noh
When are you going home?	Quando ritorna a casa?	**kwahn**-doh ree-**tor**-nah ah **kah**-zah
This is my first time in...	Questa è la mia prima volta in...	**kweh**-stah eh lah **mee**-ah **pree**-mah **vohl**-tah een
It is (not) a tourist trap.	(Non) è una trappola per turisti.	(nohn) eh **oo**-nah trah-**poh**-lah pehr too-**ree**-stee
I'm happy here.	Sono felice qui.	**soh**-noh fay-**lee**-chay kwee

This is paradise.	**Questo è il paradiso.**	**kweh**-stoh eh eel pah-rah-**dee**-zoh
The Italians are friendly.	**Gli italiani sono amichevoli.**	**lee**yee ee-tah-leeah-nee **soh**-noh ah-mee-kay-**voh**-lee
Italy is fantastic.	**L'Italia è fantastica.**	lee-**tahl**-yah eh fahn-**tah**-stee-koh
Travel is good for your health.	**Viaggiare fa bene alla salute.**	veeah-**jah**-ray fah **behn**-ay ah-lah sah-**loo**-tay
Have a good trip!	**Buon viaggio!**	bwohn veeah-joh

Map musings:

These phrases and the maps on the following pages will help you delve into family history.

I live here.	**Abito qui.**	ah-**bee**-toh kwee
I was born here.	**Sono nato[a] qui.**	**soh**-noh **nah**-toh kwee
My ancestors came from...	**I miei antenati vennero da...**	ee meeay-ee ahn-tay-**nah**-tee vay-**nay**-roh dah
I've traveled to...	**Sono stato[a] a...**	**soh**-noh **stah**-toh ah
Next I'll go to...	**Poi andrò a...**	**poh**ee ahn-**droh** ah
Where do you live?	**Dove abita?**	**doh**-vay ah-**bee**-tah
Where were you born?	**Dove è nato[a]?**	**doh**-vay eh **nah**-toh
Where did your ancestors come from?	**Da dove vennero i suoi antenati?**	dah **doh**-vay vay-**nay**-roh ee **swoh**-ee ahn-tay-**nah**-tee
Where have you traveled?	**Dove è stato[a]?**	**doh**-vay eh **stah**-toh
Where are you going?	**Dove va?**	**doh**-vay vah
Where would you like to go?	**Dove vorrebbe andare?**	**doh**-vay voh-**ray**-bay ahn-**dah**-ray

Italy

Create your own conversation:

Mix and match these words into a conversation, and make it as deep or silly as you want.

Who:

I / you	io / Lei	eeoh / lehee
he / she	lui / lei	lwee / lehee
we / they	noi / loro	nohee / loh-roh
my / your...	mio / suo...	mee-oh / soo-oh
...parents / children	...genitori / figli	jay-nee-toh-ree / feel-yee
men / women	uomini / donne	woh-mee-nee / don-nay
rich / poor	ricchi / poveri	ree-kee / poh-vay-ree
politicians	politici	poh-lee-tee-chee
big business	grande affare	grahn-day ah-fah-ray
mafia	mafia	mah-feeah
military	militare	mee-lee-tah-ray
the Italians	gli italiani	leeyee ee-tah-leeah-nee
the French	i francesi	ee frahn-chay-zee
the Germans	i tedeschi	ee tay-dehs-kee
the Americans	gli americani	leeyee ah-may-ree-kah-nee
liberals	liberali	lee-bay-rah-lee
conservatives	conservatori	kohn-sehr-vah-toh-ree
radicals	radicali	rah-dee-kah-lee
travelers	viaggiatori	veeah-jah-toh-ree
everyone	tutti	too-tee
God	Dio	deeoh

What:

want	**volere**	voh-**lay**-ray
need	**aver bisogno**	**ah**-vehr bee-**zohn**-yoh
take / give	**prendere / dare**	**prehn**-day-ray / **dah**-ray
love / hate	**amare / odiare**	ah-**mah**-ray / oh-deeah-ray
work / play	**lavorare / giocare**	lah-voh-**rah**-ray / joh-**kah**-ray
have / lack	**avere / non avere**	ah-**vay**-ray / nohn ah-**vay**-ray
learn / fear	**imparare / temere**	eem-pah-**rah**-ray / tay-**may**-ray
help / abuse	**aiutare / abusare**	ah-yoo-**tah**-ray / ah-boo-**zah**-ray
prosper / suffer	**prosperare / soffrire**	proh-spay-**rah**-ray / soh-**free**-ray
buy / sell	**comprare / vendere**	kohm-**prah**-ray / vehn-**day**-ray

Why:

love / sex	**amore / sesso**	ah-**moh**-ray / **sehs**-soh
money	**denaro**	day-**nah**-roh
power	**potere**	poh-**tay**-ray
work	**lavoro**	lah-**voh**-roh
food	**cibo**	**chee**-boh
family	**famiglia**	fah-**meel**-yah
health	**salute**	sah-**loo**-tay
hope	**speranza**	spay-**rahnt**-sah
education	**educazione**	ay-doo-kaht-see**oh**-nay
guns	**armi**	**ar**-mee
religion	**religione**	ray-lee-**joh**-nay
happiness	**felicità**	fay-lee-chee-**tah**
marijuana	**marijuana**	mah-ree-**wahn**-nah
democracy	**democrazia**	day-moh-kraht-**see**-ah

taxes	**tasse**	**tah**-say
lies	**bugie**	boo-**jee**-ay
corruption	**corruzione**	kor-root-seeoh-nay
pollution	**inquinamento**	een-kwee-nah-**mayn**-toh
television	**televisione**	tay-lay-vee-zeeoh-nay
relaxation	**rilassamento**	ree-lah-sah-**mayn**-toh
violence	**violenza**	vee-oh-**lehnt**-sah
racism	**razzismo**	raht-**seez**-moh
respect	**rispetto**	ree-**spay**-toh
war / peace	**guerra / pace**	**gwehr**-rah / **pah**-chay
global perspective	**prospettiva globale**	proh-spay-**tee**-vah gloh-**bah**-lay

You be the judge:

(no) problem	**(non c'è) problema**	(nohn chay) proh-**blay**-mah
(not) good	**(non) bene**	(nohn) **behn**-ay
(not) dangerous	**(non) pericoloso**	(nohn) pay-ree-koh-**loh**-zoh
(not) fair	**(non) giusto**	(nohn) **joo**-stoh
(not) guilty	**(non) colpevole**	(nohn) kohl-pay-**voh**-lay
(not) powerful	**(non) potente**	(nohn) poh-**tehn**-tay
(not) stupid	**(non) stupido**	(nohn) **stoo**-pee-doh
(not) happy	**(non) felice**	(nohn) fay-**lee**-chay
because / for	**perchè / per**	pehr-**keh** / pehr
and / or / from	**e / o / da**	ay / oh / dah
too much	**troppo**	**trop**-poh
enough	**abbastanza**	ah-bah-**stahnt**-sah
never enough	**mai abbastanza**	mahee ah-bah-**stahnt**-sah
worse / better	**peggio / meglio**	**peh**-joh / **mehl**-yoh

| same | **stesso** | **stay**-soh |
| here / everywhere | **qui / ovunque** | kwee / oh-**voon**-kway |

Assorted beginnings and endings:

I like...	**Mi piace...**	mee peeah-chay
I don't like...	**Non mi piace...**	nohn mee peeah-chay
Do you like...?	**Le piace...?**	lay peeah-chay
When I was young...	**Quando ero più giovane...**	**kwahn**-doh **ay**-roh pew joh-**vah**-nay
I am / Are you...?	**Sono / È...?**	**soh**-noh / eh
...an optimist / pessimist	**...ottimista / pessimista**	ot-tee-**mee**-stah / pay-see-**mee**-stah
I believe...	**Credo...**	**kray**-doh
I don't believe...	**Non credo...**	nohn **kray**-doh
Do you believe...?	**Lei crede...?**	lehee **kray**-day
...in God	**...in Dio**	een deeoh
...in life after death	**...nella vita ultraterrena**	**nay**-lah **vee**-tah ool-trah-tay-**ray**-nah
...in extraterrestrial life	**...negli extraterrestri**	**nayl**-yee ehk-strah-tehr-**rehs**-tree
...in Santa Claus	**...in Babbo Natale**	een **bah**-boh nah-**tah**-lay
Yes. / No.	**Sì. / No.**	see / noh
Maybe. / I don't know.	**Forse. / Non lo so.**	**for**-say / nohn loh soh
What's most important in life?	**Qual'è la cosa più importante nella vita?**	kwah-**leh** lah **koh**-zah pew eem-por-**tahn**-tay **nay**-lah **vee**-tah

The problem is...	Il problema è...	eel proh-**blay**-mah eh
The answer is...	La risposta è...	lah ree-**spoh**-stah eh
We have solved the world's problems.	Abbiamo risolto i problemi del mondo.	ah-beeah-moh ree-**zohl**-toh ee proh-**blay**-mee dayl **mohn**-doh

Weather:

What's the weather tomorrow?	Come sarà il tempo domani?	**koh**-may sah-**rah** eel **tehm**-poh doh-**mah**-nee
sunny / cloudy	bello / nuvoloso	**behl** loh / noo-voh-**loh**-zoh
hot / cold	caldo / freddo	**kahl**-doh / **fray**-doh
muggy / windy	umido / ventoso	oo-**mee**-doh / vehn-**toh**-zoh
rain / snow	pioggia / neve	peeoh-jah / **nay**-vay

An Italian romance:

Words of love:

I / me / you	Io / mi / ti	**ee**oh / mee / tee
flirt	flirtare	fleer-**tah**-ray
kiss	bacio	**bah**-choh
hug	abbraccio	ah-**brah**-choh
love	amore	ah-**moh**-ray
make love	fare l'amore	**fah**-ray lah-**moh**-ray
condom	preservativo	pray-zehr-vah-**tee**-voh
contraceptive	contraccetivo	kohn-trah-chay-**tee**-voh
safe sex	sesso sicuro	**sehs**-soh see-**koo**-roh
sexy	sensuale	sayn-sooah-lay

cozy	**accogliente**	ah-kohl-**yehn**-tay
romantic	**romantico**	roh-**mahn**-tee-koh
honey bunch	**dolce come il miele**	**dohl**-chay **koh**-may eel meeay-lay
cupcake	**pasticcino**	pah-stee-**chee**-noh
sugar pie	**zuccherino**	tsoo-kay-**ree**-noh
pussy cat	**gattino[a]**	gah-**tee**-noh

Ah, amore:

What's the matter?	**Qual'è il problema?**	kwah-**leh** eel proh-**blay**-mah
Nothing.	**Niente.**	neeehn-tay
I am / Are you...?	**Sono / È...?**	**soh**-noh / eh
...straight	**...normale**	nor-**mah**-lay
...gay	**...gay**	gay
...undecided	**...indeciso[a]**	een-day-**chee**-zoh
...prudish	**...pudico[a]**	**poo**-dee-koh
...horny	**...allupato[a]**	ah-loo-**pah**-toh
We are on our honeymoon.	**Siamo in luna di miele.**	seeah-moh een **loo**-nah dee meeay-lay
I have a boy friend / a girl friend.	**Ho il ragazzo / la ragazza.**	oh eel rah-**gaht**-soh / lah rah-**gaht**-sah
I'm married.	**Sono sposato[a].**	**soh**-noh spoh-**zah**-toh
I'm not married.	**Non sono sposato[a].**	nohn **soh**-noh spoh-**zah**-toh
I'm rich and single.	**Sono ricco[a] e single.**	**soh**-noh **ree**-koh ay **seeng**-glay
I'm lonely.	**Sono solo[a].**	**soh**-noh **soh**-loh
I have no diseases.	**Non ho malattie.**	nohn oh mah-lah-**tee**-ay
I have many diseases.	**Ho molte malattie.**	oh **mohl**-tay mah-lah-**tee**-ay

Can I see you again?	**Ti posso rivedere?**	tee **pos**-soh ree-vay-**day**-ray
You are my most beautiful souvenir.	**Sei il mio più bel ricordo.**	**seh**ee eel **mee**-oh pew behl ree-**kor**-doh
Is this an aphrodisiac?	**È un afrodisiaco questo?**	eh oon ah-froh-dee-**zee**-ah-koh **kweh**-stoh
This is (not) my first time.	**Questa (non) è la mia prima volta.**	**kweh**-stah (nohn) eh lah **mee**-ah **pree**-mah **vohl**-tah
Do you do this often?	**Lo fai spesso?**	loh **fah**ee **speh**-soh
How's my breath?	**Com'è il mio alito?**	koh-**meh** eel **mee**-oh ah-**lee**-toh
Let's just be friends.	**Solo amici.**	**soh**-loh ah-**mee**-chee
I'll pay for my share.	**Pago per la mia parte.**	**pah**-goh pehr lah **mee**-ah **par**-tay
Would you like a massage...?	**Vorresti un massaggio...?**	vor-**ray**-stee oon mah-**sah**-joh
...for your back	**...alla schiena**	ah-lah shee**ay**-nah
....for your feet	**....ai piedi**	**ah**ee pee**ay**-dee
Why not?	**Perchè no?**	pehr-**keh** noh
Try it.	**Provalo.**	**proh**-vah-loh
It tickles.	**Solletica.**	soh-**lay**-tee-kah
Oh my God.	**Oh mio Dio.**	oh **mee**-oh **dee**-oh
I love you.	**Ti amo.**	tee **ah**-moh
Darling, will you marry me?	**Cara, mi vuoi sposare?**	**kah**-rah mee v**woh**ee spoh-**zah**-ray

Conversing with Italian animals:

English	Italian	Pronunciation
rooster / cock-a-doodle-doo	**gallo / chicchirichì**	**gah**-loh / kee-kee-ree-**kee**
bird / tweet tweet	**uccello / cip cip**	oo-**chehl**-loh / cheep cheep
cat / meow	**gatto / miao**	**gah**-toh / **mee**-ow
dog / bark bark	**cane / bau bau**	**kah**-nay / bow bow
duck / quack quack	**oca / quac quac**	**oh**-kah / kwahk kwahk
cow / moo	**mucca / muu**	**moo**-kah / moo
pig / oink oink	**maiale / oinc oinc**	mah-**yah**-lay / oynk oynk

English-Italian Dictionary

You'll see some of the words in the dictionary listed like this: aggressivo[a]. Use the *a* ending (prounounced "ah") if you're talking about a woman.

A

above sopra
accident incidente
accountant commercialista
adaptor adattatore
address indirizzo
adult adulto
afraid spaventato[a]
after dopo
afternoon pomeriggio
aftershave dopobarba
afterwards più tardi
again ancora
age età
aggressive aggressivo[a]
agree d'accordo
AIDS AIDS
air aria
air-conditioned aria condizionata
air mail via aerea
airline aeroplano
airport aeroporto
alarm clock sveglia
alcohol alcool
allergic allergico[a]
allergies allergie
alone solo[a]

already già
always sempre
ancestor antenato[a]
ancient antico
and e
angry arrabbiato[a]
ankle caviglia
animal animale
another un altro
answer risposta
antibiotic antibiotico
antiques antichità
apartment appartamento
apology scuse
appetizers antipasti
apple mela
appointment appuntamento
approximately più o meno
arrivals arrivi
arrive arrivare
arm braccio
art arte
artificial artificiale
artist artista
ashtray portacenere
ask domandare
aspirin aspirina
at a
attractive bello[a]

DICTIONARY

aunt zia
Austria Austria
autumn autunno

B

baby bambino[a]
babysitter bambinaia
backpack zainetto
bad cattivo
bag sacchetto
baggage bagaglio
bakery panificio
balcony balcone
ball palla
banana banana
band-aid cerotto
bank banca
barber barbiere
basement seminterrato
basket cestino
bath bagno
bathroom bagno
bathtub vasca da bagno
battery batteria
beach spiaggia
beard barba
beautiful bello[a]
because perchè
bed letto
bedroom camera da letto
bedsheet lenzuolo
beef manzo
beer birra
before prima
begin cominciare

behind dietro
below sotto
belt cintura
best il migliore
better meglio
bib bavaglino
bicycle bicicletta
big grande
bill (payment) conto
bird uccello
birthday compleanno
bite (n) morso
black nero
blanket coperta
blond biondo[a]
blood sangue
blouse camicetta
blue blu
boat barca
body corpo
boiled bollito
bomb bomba
book libro
book shop libreria
boots stivali
border frontiera
borrow prendere in prestito
boss capo
bottle bottiglia
bottom fondo
bowl boccia
box scatola
boy ragazzo
bra reggiseno
bracelet braccialetto
bread pane
breakfast colazione

bridge   ponte
briefs   mutandoni
Britain   Britannia
broken   rotto
brother   fratello
brown   marrone
bucket   secchio
building   edificio
bulb   bulbo
burn (n)   bruciatura
bus   autobus
business   affari
business card   biglietto da visita
button   bottone
buy   comprare
by (via)   in

C

calendar   calendario
calorie   calorie
camera   macchina fotografica
camping   campeggio
can (n)   lattina
can (v)   potere
can opener   apriscatola
Canada   Canada
canal   canale
candle   candela
candy   caramella
canoe   canoa
cap   berretto
captain   capitano
car   macchina
carafe   caraffa
card   cartina

cards (deck)   carte
careful   prudente
carpet   tappeto
carry   portare
cashier   cassiere
cassette   cassetta
castle   castello
cat   gatto
catch (v)   prendere
cathedral   cattedrale
cave   grotta
cellar   cantina
center   centro
century   secolo
chair   sedia
change (v)   cambiare
change (n)   cambio
charming   affascinante
cheap   economico
check   assegno
Cheers!   Salute!
cheese   formaggio
chicken   pollo
children   bambini
Chinese (adj)   cinese
chocolate   cioccolato
Christmas   Natale
church   chiesa
cigarette   sigarette
cinema   cinema
city   città
class   classe
clean (adj)   pulito
clear   chiaro
cliff   dirupo
closed   chiuso
cloth   stoffa

DICTIONARY

clothes vestiti
clothes pins spilla
clothesline marca
cloudy nuvoloso
coast costa
coat hanger appendiabiti
coffee caffè
coins monete
cold (adj) freddo
colors colori
comb (n) pettine
come venire
comfortable confortevole
compact disc compact disc
complain protestare
complicated complicato
computer computer
concert concerto
condom preservativo
conductor conduttore
confirm confermare
congratulations congratulazioni
connection (train) coincidenza
constipation stitichezza
cook (v) cucinare
cool fresco
cork tappo
corkscrew cavatappi
corner angolo
corridor corridoio
cost (v) costare
cot lettino
cotton cotone
cough (v) tossire
cough drop sciroppo
country paese
countryside campagna

cousin cugino[a]
cow mucca
cozy confortevole
crafts arte
cream panna
credit card carta di credito
crowd (n) folla
cry (v) piangere
cup tazza

D

dad papà
dance (v) ballare
danger pericolo
dangerous pericoloso
dark scuro
daughter figlia
day giorno
dead morto
delay ritardo
delicious delizioso
dental floss filo interdentale
dentist dentista
deodorant deodorante
depart partire
departures partenze
deposit deposito
dessert dolci
detour deviazione
diabetic diabetico[a]
diamond diamante
diaper pannolino
diarrhea diarrea
dictionary dizionario
die morire

difficult difficile
dinner cena
direct diretto
direction direzione
dirty sporco
discount sconto
disease malattia
disturb disturbare
divorced divorziato[a]
doctor dottore
dog cane
doll bambola
donkey asino
door porta
dormitory camerata
double doppio
down giù
dream (v) sognare
dream (n) sogno
dress (n) vestito
drink (n) bevanda
drive (v) guidare
driver autista
drunk ubriaco
dry secco, asciutto

E

each ogni
ear orecchio
early presto
earplugs tappi per le orecchie
earrings orecchini
earth terra
east est
Easter Pasqua

easy facile
eat mangiare
elbow gomito
elevator ascensore
embarrassing imbarazzante
embassy ambasciata
empty vuoto
engineer ingeniere
English inglese
enjoy divertirsi
enough abbastanza
entrance ingresso
entry entrata
envelope busta
eraser gomma da cancellare
especially specialmente
Europe Europa
evening sera
every ogni
everything tutto
exactly esattamente
example esempio
excellent eccellente
except eccetto
exchange (n) cambio
excuse me mi scusi
exhausted esausto
exit uscita
expensive caro
explain spiegare
eye occhio

F

face faccia
factory fabbrica

fall (v) cadere
false falso
family famiglia
famous famoso[a]
fantastic fantastico[a]
far lontano
farm fattoria
farmer contadino[a]
fashion moda
fat (adj) grasso[a]
father padre
faucet rubinetto
fax fax
female femmina
ferry traghetto
fever febbre
few poco
field campo
fight (v) combattere
fight (n) lotta
fine (good) bene
finger dito
finish (v) finire
fireworks fuochi d'artificio
first primo
first aid primo soccorso
first class prima classe
fish (v) pescare
fish pesce
fix (v) aggiustare
fizzy frizzante
flag bandiera
flashlight torcia
flavor (n) aroma
flea pulce
flight volo
flower fiore

flu influenza
fly volare
fog nebbia
food cibo
foot piede
football calcio
for per
forbidden vietato
foreign straniero
forget dimenticare
fork forchetta
fountain fontana
France Francia
free (no cost) gratis
fresh fresco
Friday venerdì
friend amico
friendship amicizia
frisbee frisbee
from da
fruit frutta
fun divertimento
funeral funerale
funny divertente
furniture mobili
future futuro

G

gallery galleria
game gioco
garage garage
garden giardino
gardening giardinaggio
gas benzina
gas station benzinaio

gay omosessuale
gentleman signore
genuine genuino
Germany Germania
gift regalo
girl ragazza
give dare
glass bicchiere
glasses (eye) occhiali
gloves guanti
go andare
go through attraversare
God Dio
gold oro
golf golf
good buono
good day buon giorno
goodbye arrivederci
grammar grammatica
grandchild nipote
grandfather nonno
grandmother nonna
gray grigio
greasy grasso
great ottimo
Greece Grecia
green verde
grocery store alimentari
guarantee garantito
guest ospite
guide guida
guidebook guida
guitar chitarra
gum gomma da masticare
gun pistola

H

hair capelli
haircut taglio di capelli
hand mano
handicapped andicappato
handicrafts artigianato
handle (n) manico
handsome attraente
happy contento[a]
harbor porto
hard duro
hat cappello
hate (v) odiare
have avere
he lui
head testa
headache mal di testa
healthy sano
hear udire
heart cuore
heat (n) calore
heat (v) scaldare
heaven paradiso
heavy pesante
hello ciao
help aiutare
help (n) aiuto
hemorrhoids emorroidi
here qui
hi ciao
high alto
highchair seggiolone
highway autostrada
hike fare una gita
hill collina

history storia
hitchhike autostop
hobby hobby
hole buco
holiday giorno festivo
homemade casalingo
homesick nostalgico[a]
honest onesto[a]
honeymoon luna di miele
horrible orribile
horse cavallo
horse riding equitazione
hospital ospedale
hot caldo
hotel hotel
hour ora
house casa
how come
how many quanti
how much ($) quanto costa
hungry affamato
hurry (v) avere fretta
husband marito
hydrofoil aliscafo

in in
included incluso
incredible incredibile
independent indipendente
indigestion indigestione
industry industria
information informazioni
injured infortunato
innocent innocente
insect insetto
insect repellant lozione anti-zanzare
inside dentro
instant istante
instead invece
insurance assicurazione
intelligent intelligente
interesting interessante
invitation invito
iodine iodio
is è
island isola
Italy Italia
itch (n) prurito

I

I io
ice ghiaccio
ice cream gelato
if se
ill malato[a]
immediately immediatamente
important importante
imported importato
impossible impossibile

J

jacket giubbotto
jaw mascella
jeans jeans
jewelry gioielleria
job lavoro
jogging footing
joke (n) scherzo
journey viaggio
juice succo

jump (v) saltare

K

keep tenere
kettle bollitore
key chiave
kill uccidere
kind gentile
king re
kiss bacio
kitchen cucina
knee ginocchio
knife coltello
know sapere

L

ladder scala
ladies signore
lake lago
lamb agnello
language lingua
large grande
last ultimo
late tardi
later più tardi
laugh (v) ridere
laundromat lavanderia
lawyer avvocato
lazy pigro[a]
leather pelle
leave partire
left sinistra
leg gamba
lend prestare

letter lettera
library biblioteca
life vita
light (n) luce
light bulb lampadina
lighter (n) accendino
like (v) piacere
lip labbro
list lista
listen ascoltare
liter litro
little (adj) piccolo
live (v) vivoro
local locale
lock (v) chiudere
lock (n) serratura
lockers armadietti
look guardare
lost perso[a]
loud forte
love (v) amare
lover amante
low basso
lozenges pastiglie per la gola
luck fortuna
luggage bagaglio
lukewarm tiepido
lungs polmoni

M

macho macho
mad arrabbiato[a]
magazine rivista
mail (n) posta
main principale

DICTIONARY

make (v) fare
male maschio
man uomo
manager direttore
many molti
map cartina
market mercato
married sposato[a]
matches fiammiferi
maximum massimo
maybe forse
meat carne
medicine medicina
medium medio
men uomini
menu menù
message messaggio
metal metallo
midnight mezzanotte
mineral water acqua minerale
minimum minimo
minutes minuti
mirror specchio
Miss Signorina
mistake errore
misunderstanding
  incomprensione
mix (n) misto
modern moderno
moment momento
Monday lunedì
money soldi
month mese
monument monumento
moon luna
more ancora
morning mattina

mosquito zanzara
mother madre
mother-in-law suocera
mountain montagna
moustache baffi
mouth bocca
movie film
Mr. Signore
Mrs. Signora
much molto
muscle muscolo
museum museo
music musica
my mio / mia

N

nail clipper tagliaunghie
naked nudo[a]
name nome
napkin salvietta
narrow stretto
nationality nazionalità
natural naturale
nature natura
nausea nausea
near vicino
necessary necessario
necklace collana
need avere bisogno di
needle ago
nephew nipote
nervous nervoso[a]
never mai
new nuovo
newspaper giornale

next prossimo
nice bello[a]
niece nipote
nickname soprannome
night notte
no no
no vacancy completo
noisy rumoroso[a]
non-smoking vietato fumare
noon mozzogiorno
normal normale
north nord
nose naso
not non
notebook blocco note
nothing niente
now adesso

O

occupation lavoro
occupied occupato
ocean oceano
of di
office ufficio
oil (n) olio
OK d'accordo
old vecchio[a]
on su
once una volta
one way (street) senso unico
one way (ticket) andata
only solo
open (adj) aperto
open (v) aprire
opera opera

operator centralinista
optician ottico
or o
orange (color) arancione
orange (fruit) arancia
original originale
other altro
outdoors all'aria aperta
oven forno
over (finished) finito
own (v) possedere
owner padrone

P

pacifier succhiotto
package pacco
page pagina
pail secchio
pain dolore
painting quadro
palace palazzo
panties mutande
pants pantaloni
paper carta
paper clip graffetta
parents genitori
park (v) parcheggiare
park (garden) parco
party festa
passenger passeggero[a]
passport passaporto
pay pagare
peace pace
pedestrian pedone
pen penna

pencil   matita
people   persone
pepper   pepe
percent   percentuale
perfect   perfetto
perfume   profumo
period (of time)   periodo
period (woman's)   mestruazioni
person   persona
pet (n)   animale domestico
pharmacy   farmacia
photo   foto
photocopy   fotocopia
pick-pocket   borsaiolo
picnic   picnic
piece   pezzo
pig   maiale
pill   pillola
pillow   cuscino
pin   spilla
pink   rosa
pity, it's a   che peccato
pizza   pizza
plain   semplice
plane   aereoplano
plant   pianta
plastic   plastica
plastic bag   sacchetto di plastica
plate   piatto
platform (train)   binario
play (v)   giocare
play   teatro
please   per favore
pliers   pinzette
pocket   tasca
point (v)   indicare
police   polizia

poor   povero
pork   porco
possible   possibile
postcard   cartolina
poster   poster
practical   pratico[a]
pregnant   incinta
prescription   prescrizione
present (gift)   regalo
pretty   carino[a]
price   prezzo
priest   prete
private   privato
problem   problema
profession   professione
prohibited   proibito
pronunciation   pronuncia
public   pubblico
pull   tirare
purple   viola
purse   borsa
push   spingere

Q

quality   qualità
quarter (¼)   quarto
queen   regina
question (n)   domanda
quiet   tranquillo

R

R.V.   camper
rabbit   coniglio
radio   radio

raft gommone
railway rotaie
rain (n) pioggia
rainbow arcobaleno
raincoat impermeabile
rape (n) violenza carnale
raw crudo
razor rasoio
ready pronto
receipt ricevuta
receive ricevere
receptionist centralinista
recipe ricetta
recommend raccomandare
red rosso
refill (v) riempire
refund (n) rimborso
relax (v) riposare
religion religione
remember ricordare
rent (v) affittare
repair (v) riparare
reserve prenotare
reservation prenotazione
return ritornare
rich ricco[a]
right destra
ring (n) anello
ripe maturo
river fiume
rock (n) pietra
roller skates pattini a rotelle
romantic romantico[a]
roof tetto
room camera
rope corda
rotten marcio

round trip ritorno
rowboat barca a remi
rucksack zaino
rug tappeto
ruins rovine
run (v) correre

S

sad triste
safe sicuro
safety pin spilla da balia
sailing vela
sale liquidazione
same stesso
sandals sandali
sandwich panino
sanitary napkins assorbenti igienici
Saturday sabato
scandalous scandaloso
scarf sciarpa
school scuola
science scienza
scientist scienziato[a]
scissors forbici
scotch tape nastro adesivo
screwdriver cacciaviti
sculptor scultore
sculpture scultura
sea mare
seafood frutti di mare
seat posto
second class secondo classe
secret segreto
see vedere

self-service self-service
sell vendere
send spedire
separate (adj) separato
serious serio
service servizio
sex sesso
sexy sexy
shampoo shampoo
shaving cream crema da barba
she lei
sheet lenzuolo
shell conchiglia
ship (n) nave
shirt camicia
shoes scarpe
shopping fare spese
short corto[a]
shorts pantaloncini
shoulder spalle
show (v) mostrare
show (n) spettacolo
shower doccia
shy timido[a]
sick malato[a]
sign segno
signature firma
silence silenzio
silk seta
silver argento
similar simile
simple semplice
sing cantare
singer cantante
single (m / f) scapolo / nubile
sink lavandino
sir signore

sister sorella
size taglia
skating pattinaggio
ski (v) sciare
skin pelle
skinny magro[a]
skirt gonna
sky cielo
sleep (v) dormire
sleepy assonnato[a]
slice fettina
slide (photo) diapositiva
slippery scivoloso
slow lento
small piccolo[a]
smell (n) odore
smile (n) sorriso
smoking fumare
snack merendina
sneeze (n) starnuto
snore russare
soap sapone
soccer calcio
socks calzini
something qualcosa
son figlio
song canzone
soon subito
sorry mi dispiace
sour acerbo
south sud
speak parlare
specialty specialità
speed velocità
spend spendere
spider ragno
spoon cucchiaio

sport sport
spring primavera
square piazza
stapler pinzatrice
stairs scale
stamps francobolli
star (in sky) stella
state stato
station stazione
stomach stomaco
stop (v) fermare
stop (n) stop / alt
storm temporale
story (floor) storia
straight dritto
strange (odd) strano[a]
stream (n) corrente
street strada
strike (stop work) sciopero
string filo
strong forte
stuck incastrato
student studente
stupid stupido[a]
sturdy resistente
style stile
suddenly improvvisamente
suitcase valigia
summer estate
sun sole
sunbathe abbronzarsi
sunburn bruciatura del sole
Sunday domenica
sunglasses occhiali da sole
sunny assolato
sunset tramonto
sunscreen protezione solare

sunshine sole
sunstroke insolazione
suntan (n) abbronzatura
suntan lotion crema per il sole
supermarket supermercato
supplement supplemento
surprise (n) sorpresa
swallow (v) ingoiare
sweat (v) sudare
sweater maglione
sweet dolce
swim nuotare
swim trunks costume da bagno
swimming pool piscina
swimsuit costume da bagno
Switzerland Svizzera
synthetic sintetico

T

table tavolo
tail coda
take prendere
take out (food) portar via
talcum powder borotalco
talk parlare
tall alto
tampons assorbenti interni
tape (cassette) cassetta
taste (v) assaggiare
taste (n) gusto
tax tasse
teacher insegnante
team squadra
teenager adolescente
telephone telefono

television televisione
temperature temperatura
tender tenero
tennis tennis
tennis shoes scarpe da tennis
tent tenda
tent pegs picchetti della tenda
terrible terribile
thanks grazie
theater teatro
thermometer termometro
thick spesso
thief ladro
thigh coscia
thin sottile
thing cosa
think pensare
thirsty assetato
thongs sandali infradito
thread filo
throat gola
through attraverso
throw tirare
Thursday giovedì
ticket biglietto
tight stretto
timetable orario
tired stanco
tissues fazzolettini
to a
today oggi
toe dito del piede
together insieme
toilet toilette
toilet paper carta igienica
tomorrow domani
tonight stanotte

too troppo
tooth dente
toothbrush spazzolino da denti
toothpaste dentifricio
toothpick stuzzicadenti
total totale
tour giro
tourist turista
towel asciugamano
tower torre
town città
toy giocattolo
track (train) binario
traditional tradizionale
traffic traffico
train treno
translate tradurre
travel viaggiare
travel agency agenzia di viaggi
traveler's check traveler's
  check
tree albero
trip viaggio
trouble guaio
T-shirt maglietta
Tuesday martedì
tunnel tunnel
tweezers pinzette
twins gemelli

U

ugly brutto[a]
umbrella ombrello
uncle zio
under sotto

underpants mutandine
understand capire
underwear mutande
unemployed disoccupato[a]
unfortunately sfortunatamente
United States Stati Uniti
university università
up su
upstairs di sopra
urgent urgente
us noi
use usare

V

vacancy (hotel) camare libere
vacant libero
valley valle
vegetarian (n) vegetariano[a]
very molto
vest panciotto
video video
video camera video camera
video recorder video registratore
view vista
village villaggio
vineyard vigneto
virus virus
visit (n) visita
visit (v) visitare
vitamins vitamine
voice voce
vomit (v) vomitare

W

waist vita
wait aspettare
waiter cameriere
waitress cameriera
wake up svegliarsi
walk (v) camminare
wallet portafoglio
want volere
warm (adj) caldo
wash lavare
watch (v) guardare
watch (n) orologio
water acqua
water, tap acqua del rubinetto
waterfall cascata
we noi
weather tempo
weather forecast previsioni del tempo
wedding matrimonio
Wednesday mercoledì
week settimana
weight peso
welcome benvenuto
west ovest
wet bagnato
what che cosa
wheel ruota
when quando
where dove
whipped cream panna
white bianco
white-out bianchetto
who chi

DICTIONARY

why perchè
widow vedova
widower vedovo
wife moglie
wild selvaggio[a]
wind vento
window finestra
wine vino
wing ala
winter inverno
wish (v) desiderare
with con
without senza
women donne
wood legno
wool lana
word parola
work (v) lavorare
work (n) lavoro
world mondo
worse peggio
worst peggiore
wrap incartare
wrist polso
write scrivere

Y

year anno
yellow giallo
yes si
yesterday ieri
you (formal) Lei
you (informal) tu
young giovane

youth hostel ostello della
  gioventù

Z

zero zero
zip-lock bag busta de plastica
  sigillabile
zipper chiusura lampo
zoo zoo

Italian-English Dictionary

You'll see some of the words in the dictionary listed like this: aggressivo[a]. Use the *a* ending (prounounced "ah") if you're talking about a woman.

A

a at
a to
abbastanza enough
abbronzarsi sunbathe
abbronzatura suntan (n)
accendino lighter (n)
acerbo sour
acqua water
acqua del rubinetto water, tap
acqua minerale mineral water
adattatore adaptor
adesso now
adolescente teenager
adulto adult
aeroplano plane
aeroporto airport
affamato hungry
affari business
affascinante charming
affittare rent (v)
agenzia di viaggi travel agency
aggiustare fix (v)
aggressivo[a] aggressive
agnello lamb
ago needle
AIDS AIDS
aiutare help
aiuto help (n)

ala wing
albero tree
alcool alcohol
alimentari grocery store
aliscafo hydrofoil
all'aria aperta outdoors
allergico[a] allergic
allergie allergies
alto high
alto tall
altro other
amante lover
amare love (v)
ambasciata embassy
amicizia friendship
amico friend
ancora again
ancora more
andare go
andata one way (ticket)
andicappato handicapped
anello ring (n)
angolo corner
animale animal
animale domestico pet (n)
anno year
antenato[a] ancestor
antibiotico antibiotic
antichità antiques
antico ancient

antipasti appetizers
aperto open (adj)
appartamento apartment
appendiabiti coat hanger
appuntamento appointment
aprire open (v)
apriscatola can opener
arancia orange (fruit)
arancione orange (color)
arcobaleno rainbow
argento silver
aria air
aria condizionata air-conditioned
armadietti lockers
aroma flavor (n)
arrabbiato[a] angry
arrabbiato[a] mad
arrivare arrive
arrivederci goodbye
arrivi arrivals
arte art
arte crafts
artificiale artificial
artigianato handicrafts
artista artist
ascensore elevator
asciugamano towel
ascoltare listen
asino donkey
aspettare wait
aspirina aspirin
assaggiare taste (v)
assegno check
assetato thirsty
assicurazione insurance
assolato sunny
assonnato[a] sleepy

assorbenti igienici sanitary napkins
assorbenti interni tampons
attraente handsome
attraversare go through
attraverso through
Austria Austria
autista driver
autobus bus
autostop hitchhike
autostrada highway
autunno autumn
avere have
avere bisogno di need
avere fretta hurry (v)
avvocato lawyer

B

bacio kiss
baffi moustache
bagaglio baggage
bagaglio luggage
bagnato wet
bagno bath
bagno bathroom
balcone balcony
ballare dance (v)
bambinaia babysitter
bambini children
bambino[a] baby
bambola doll
banana banana
banca bank
bandiera flag
barba beard
barbiere barber

barca   boat
barca a remi   rowboat
basso   low
batteria   battery
bavaglino   bib
bello[a]   attractive
bello[a]   beautiful
bello[a]   nice
bene   fine (good)
benvenuto   welcome
benzina   gas
benzinaio   gas station
berretto   cap
bevanda   drink (n)
bianchetto   white-out
bianco   white
biblioteca   library
bicchiere   glass
bicicletta   bicycle
biglietto   ticket
biglietto da visita   business card
binario   platform (train)
binario   track (train)
biondo[a]   blond
birra   beer
blocco note   notebook
blu   blue
bocca   mouth
boccia   bowl
bollito   boiled
bollitore   kettle
bomba   bomb
borotalco   talcum powder
borsa   purse
borsaiolo   pick-pocket
bottiglia   bottle
bottone   button

braccialetto   bracelet
braccio   arm
Britannia   Britain
bruciatura   burn (n)
bruciatura del sole   sunburn
brutto[a]   ugly
buco   hole
bulbo   bulb
buon giorno   good day
buono   good
busta   envelope
busta de plastica sigillabile
   zip-lock bag

C

cacciaviti   screwdriver
cadere   fall (v)
caffè   coffee
calcio   football
calcio   soccer
caldo   hot
caldo   warm (adj)
calendario   calendar
calore   heat (n)
calorie   calorie
calzini   socks
camare libere   vacancy (hotel)
cambiare   change (v)
cambio   change (n)
cambio   exchange (n)
camera   room
camera da letto   bedroom
camerata   dormitory
cameriera   waitress
cameriere   waiter

camicetta blouse
camicia shirt
camminare walk (v)
campagna countryside
campeggio camping
camper R.V.
campo field
Canada Canada
canale canal
candela candle
cane dog
canoa canoe
cantante singer
cantare sing
cantina cellar
canzone song
capelli hair
capire understand
capitano captain
capo boss
cappello hat
caraffa carafe
caramella candy
carino[a] pretty
carne meat
caro expensive
carta paper
carta di credito credit card
carta igienica toilet paper
carte cards (deck)
cartina card
cartina map
cartolina postcard
casa house
casalingo homemade
cascata waterfall
cassetta cassette

cassetta tape (cassette)
cassiere cashier
castello castle
cattedrale cathedral
cattivo bad
cavallo horse
cavatappi corkscrew
caviglia ankle
cena dinner
centralinista operator
centralinista receptionist
centro center
cerotto band-aid
cestino basket
che cosa what
che peccato pity, it's a
chi who
chiaro clear
chiave key
chiesa church
chitarra guitar
chiudere lock (v)
chiuso closed
chiusura lampo zipper
ciao hello
ciao hi
cibo food
cielo sky
cinema cinema
cinese Chinese (adj)
cintura belt
cioccolato chocolate
città city
città town
classe class
coda tail
coincidenza connection (train)

colazione   breakfast
collana   necklace
collina   hill
colori   colors
coltello   knife
combattere   fight (v)
come   how
cominciare   begin
commercialista   accountant
compact disc   compact disc
compleanno   birthday
completo   no vacancy
complicato   complicated
comprare   buy
computer   computer
con   with
concerto   concert
conchiglia   shell
conduttore   conductor
confermare   confirm
confortevol   comfortable
confortevole   cozy
congratulazioni   congratulations
coniglio   rabbit
contadino[a]   farmer
contento[a]   happy
conto   bill (payment)
coperta   blanket
corda   rope
corpo   body
corrente   stream (n)
correre   run (v)
corridoio   corridor
corto[a]   short
cosa   thing
coscia   thigh
costa   coast

costare   cost (v)
costume da bagno   swimsuit
costume de bagno   swim trunks
cotone   cotton
crema da barba   shaving cream
crema per il sole   suntan lotion
crudo   raw
cucchiaio   spoon
cucina   kitchen
cucinare   cook (v)
cugino[a]   cousin
cuore   heart
cuscino   pillow

D

da   from
d'accordo   agree
d'accordo   OK
dare   give
delizioso   delicious
dente   tooth
dentifricio   toothpaste
dentista   dentist
dentro   inside
deodorante   deodorant
deposito   deposit
desiderare   wish (v)
destra   right
deviazione   detour
di   of
di sopra   upstairs
diabetico[a]   diabetic
diamante   diamond
diapositiva   slide (photo)
diarrea   diarrhea

dietro behind
difficile difficult
dimenticare forget
Dio God
diretto direct
direttore manager
direzione direction
dirupo cliff
disoccupato[a] unemployed
disturbare disturb
dito finger
dito del piede toe
divertente funny
divertimento fun
divertirsi enjoy
divorziato[a] divorced
dizionario dictionary
doccia shower
dolce sweet
dolci dessert
dolore pain
domanda question (n)
domandare ask
domani tomorrow
domenica Sunday
donne women
dopo after
dopobarba aftershave
doppio double
dormire sleep (v)
dottore doctor
dove where
dritto straight
duro hard

E

e and
è is
eccellente excellent
eccetto except
economico cheap
edificio building
entrata entry
equitazione horse riding
errore mistake
esattamente exactly
esausto exhausted
esempio example
est east
estate summer
età age
Europa Europe

F

fabbrica factory
faccia face
facile easy
falso false
famiglia family
famoso[a] famous
fantastico[a] fantastic
fare make (v)
fare spese shopping
fare una gita hike
farmacia pharmacy
fattoria farm
fax fax
fazzolettini tissues
febbre fever

femmina female
fermare stop (v)
festa party
fettina slice
fiammiferi matches
figlia daughter
figlio son
film movie
filo string
filo thread
filo interdentale dental floss
finestra window
finire finish (v)
finito over (finished)
fiore flower
firma signature
fiume river
folla crowd (n)
fondo bottom
fontana fountain
footing jogging
forbici scissors
forchetta fork
formaggio cheese
forno oven
forse maybe
forte loud
forte strong
fortuna luck
foto photo
fotocopia photocopy
Francia France
francobolli stamps
fratello brother
freddo cold (adj)
fresco cool
fresco fresh

frisbee frisbee
frizzante fizzy
frontiera border
frutta fruit
frutti di mare seafood
fumare smoking
funerale funeral
fuochi d'artificio fireworks
futuro future

G

galleria gallery
gamba leg
garage garage
garantito guarantee
gatto cat
gelato ice cream
gemelli twins
genitori parents
gentile kind
genuino genuine
Germania Germany
ghiaccio ice
già already
giallo yellow
giardinaggio gardening
giardino garden
ginocchio knee
giocare play (v)
giocattolo toy
gioco game
gioielleria jewelry
giornale newspaper
giorno day
giorno festivo holiday

giovane young
giovedì Thursday
giro tour
giù down
giubbotto jacket
gola throat
golf golf
gomito elbow
gomma da cancellare eraser
gomma da masticare gum
gommone raft
gonna skirt
graffetta paper clip
grammatica grammar
grande big
grande large
grasso greasy
grasso[a] fat (adj)
gratis free (no cost)
grazie thanks
Grecia Greece
grigio gray
grotta cave
guaio trouble
guanti gloves
guardare look
guardare watch (v)
guida guide
guida guidebook
guidare drive (v)
gusto taste (n)

H

hobby hobby
hotel hotel

I

ieri yesterday
il migliore best
imbarazzante embarrassing
immediatamente immediately
impermeabile raincoat
importante important
importato imported
impossibile impossible
improvvisamente suddenly
in by (via)
in in
incartare wrap
incastrato stuck
incidente accident
incinta pregnant
incluso included
incomprensione misunderstanding
incredibile incredible
indicare point (v)
indigestione indigestion
indipendente independent
indirizzo address
industria industry
influenza flu
informazioni information
infortunato injured
ingeniere engineer
inglese English
ingoiare swallow (v)
ingresso entrance
innocente innocent
insegnante teacher
insetto insect

insieme together
insolazione sunstroke
intelligente intelligent
interessante interesting
invece instead
inverno winter
invito invitation
io I
Iodio iodine
isola island
istante instant
Italia Italy

J

jeans jeans

L

labbro lip
ladro thief
lago lake
lampadina light bulb
lana wool
lattina can (n)
lavanderia laundromat
lavandino sink
lavare wash
lavorare work (v)
lavoro job
lavoro occupation
lavoro work (n)
legno wood
lei her
lei she
Lei you (formal)

lento slow
lenzuolo bedsheet
lenzuolo sheet
lettera letter
lettino cot
letto bed
libero vacant
librerla book shop
libro book
linea aerea airline
lingua language
liquidazione sale
lista list
litro liter
locale local
lontano far
lotta fight (n)
lozione anti-zanzare insect repellant
luce light (n)
lui he
luna moon
luna di miele honeymoon
lunedì Monday

M

macchina car
macchina fotografica camera
macho macho
madre mother
maglietta T-shirt
maglione sweater
magro[a] skinny
mai never
maiale pig

mal di testa headache
malato[a] ill
malato[a] sick
malattia disease
mangiare eat
manico handle (n)
mano hand
manzo beef
marca clothesline
marcio rotten
mare sea
marito husband
marrone brown
martedì Tuesday
mascella jaw
maschio male
massimo maximum
matita pencil
matrimonio wedding
mattina morning
maturo ripe
medicina medicine
medio medium
meglio better
mela apple
menù menu
mercato market
mercoledì Wednesday
merendina snack
mese month
messaggio message
mestruazioni period (woman's)
metallo metal
mezzanotte midnight
mezzogiorno noon
mi dispiace sorry
mi scusi excuse me

minimo minimum
minuti minutes
mio / mia my
misto mix (n)
mobili furniture
moda fashion
moderno modern
moglie wife
molti many
molto much
molto very
momento moment
mondo world
monete coins
montagna mountain
monumento monument
morire die
morso bite (n)
morto dead
mostrare show (v)
mucca cow
muscolo muscle
museo museum
musica music
mutande panties
mutande underwear
mutandine underpants
mutandoni briefs

N

naso nose
nastro adesivo scotch tape
Natale Christmas
natura nature
naturale natural

nausea nausea
nave ship (n)
nazionalità nationality
nebbia fog
necessario necessary
nero black
nervoso[a] nervous
niente nothing
nipote grandchild
nipote nephew
nipote niece
no no
noi us
noi we
nome name
non not
nonna grandmother
nonno grandfather
nord north
normale normal
nostalgico[a] homesick
notte night
nudo[a] naked
nuotare swim
nuovo new
nuvoloso cloudy

O

o or
occhiali glasses (eye)
occhiali da sole sunglasses
occhio eye
occupato occupied
oceano ocean
odiare hate (v)

odore smell (n)
oggi today
ogni each
ogni every
olio oil (n)
ombrello umbrella
omosessuale gay
onesto[a] honest
opera opera
ora hour
orario timetable
orecchini earrings
orecchio ear
originale original
oro gold
orologio watch (n)
orribile horrible
ospedale hospital
ospite guest
ostello della gioventù youth hostel
ottico optician
ottimo great
ovest west

P

pacco package
pace peace
padre father
padrone owner
paese country
pagare pay
pagina page
palazzo palace
palla ball

panciotto vest
pane bread
panificio bakery
panino sandwich
panna cream
panna whipped cream
pannolino diaper
pantaloncini shorts
pantaloni pants
papà dad
paradiso heaven
parcheggiare park (v)
parco park (garden)
parlare speak
parlare talk
parola word
partenze departures
partire depart
partire leave
Pasqua Easter
passaporto passport
passeggero[a] passenger
pastiglie per la gola lozenges
pattinaggio skating
pattini a rotelle roller skates
pedone pedestrian
peggio worse
peggiore worst
pelle leather
pelle skin
penna pen
pensare think
pepe pepper
per for
per favore please
percentuale percent
perchè because

perchè why
perfetto perfect
pericolo danger
pericoloso dangerous
periodo period (of time)
perso[a] lost
persona person
persone people
pesante heavy
pescare fish (v)
pesce fish
peso weight
pettine comb (n)
pezzo piece
piacere like (v)
piangere cry (v)
pianta plant
piatto plate
piazza square
picchetti della tenda tent pegs
piccolo little (adj)
piccolo[a] small
picnic picnic
piede foot
pietra rock (n)
pigro[a] lazy
pillola pill
pinzatrice stapler
pinzette pliers
pinzette tweezers
pioggia rain (n)
piscina swimming pool
pistola gun
più o meno approximately
più tardi afterwards
più tardi later
pizza pizza

plastica plastic
poco few
polizia police
pollo chicken
polmoni lungs
polso wrist
pomeriggio afternoon
ponte bridge
porco pork
porta door
portacenere ashtray
portafoglio wallet
portar via take out (food)
portare carry
porto harbor
possedere own (v)
possibile possible
posta mail (n)
poster poster
posto seat
potere can (v)
povero poor
pratico[a] practical
prendere catch (v)
prendere take
prendere in prestito borrow
prenotare reserve
prenotazione reservation
prescrizlone prescription
preservativo condom
prestare lend
presto early
prete priest
previsioni del tempo weather forecast
prezzo price
prima before

prima classe first class
primavera spring
primo first
primo soccorso first aid
principale main
privato private
problema problem
professione profession
profumo perfume
proibito prohibited
pronto ready
pronuncia pronunciation
prossimo next
protestare complain
protezione solare sunscreen
prudente careful
prurito itch (n)
pubblico public
pulce flea
pulito clean (adj)

Q

quadro painting
qualcosa something
qualità quality
quando when
quanti how many
quanto costa how much ($)
quarto quarter (¼)
qui here

R

raccomandare recommend
radio radio

ragazza girl
ragazzo boy
ragno spider
rasoio razor
re king
regalo gift
regalo present (gift)
reggiseno bra
regina queen
religione religion
resistente sturdy
ricco[a] rich
ricetta recipe
ricevere receive
ricevuta receipt
ricordare remember
ridere laugh (v)
riempire refill (v)
rimborso refund (n)
riparare repair (v)
riposare relax (v)
risposta answer
ritardo delay
ritornare return
ritorno round trip
rivista magazine
romantico[a] romantic
rosa pink
rosso red
rotaie railway
rotto broken
rovine ruins
rubinetto faucet
rumoroso[a] noisy
ruota wheel
russare snore

S

sabato Saturday
sacchetto bag
sacchetto di plastica plastic bag
saltare jump (v)
Salute! Cheers!
salvietta napkin
sandali sandals
sandali infradito thongs
sangue blood
sano healthy
sapere know
sapone soap
scala ladder
scaldare heat (v)
scale stairs
scandaloso scandalous
scapolo / nubile single (m / f)
scarpe shoes
scarpe da tennis tennis shoes
scatola box
scherzo joke (n)
sciare ski (v)
sciarpa scarf
scienza science
scienziato[a] scientist
sciopero strike (stop work)
sciroppo cough drop
scivoloso slippery
sconto discount
scrivere write
scultore sculptor
scultura sculpture

scuola school
scuro dark
scuse apology
se if
secchio bucket
secchio pail
secco, asciutto dry
secolo century
secondo classe second class
sedia chair
seggiolone highchair
segno sign
segreto secret
self-service self-service
selvaggio[a] wlld
seminterrato basement
semplice plain
semplice simple
sempre always
senso unico one way (street)
senza without
separato separate (adj)
sera evening
serio serious
serratura lock (n)
servizio service
sesso sex
seta silk
settimana week
sexy sexy
sfortunatamente unfortunately
shampoo shampoo
si yes
sicuro safe
sigarette cigarette
Signora Mrs.
signore gentleman

signore ladies
Signore Mr.
signore sir
Signorina Miss
silenzio silence
simile similar
sinistra left
sintetico synthetic
sognare dream (v)
sogno dream (n)
soldi money
sole sun
sole sunshine
solu[a] alone
solo only
sopra above
soprannome nickname
sorella sister
sorpresa surprise (n)
sorriso smile (n)
sottile thin
sotto below
sotto under
spalle shoulder
spaventato[a] afraid
spazzolino da denti toothbrush
specchlo mirror
specialità specialty
specialmente especially
spedire send
spendere spend
spesso thick
spettacolo show (n)
spiaggia beach
spiegare explain
spilla clothes pins
spilla pin

spilla da balia safety pin
spingere push
sporco dirty
sport sport
sposato[a] married
squadra team
stanco tired
stanotte tonight
starnuto sneeze (n)
Stati Uniti United States
stato state
stazione station
stella star (in sky)
stesso same
stile style
stitichezza constipation
stivali boots
stoffa cloth
stomaco stomach
stop / alt stop (n)
storia history
storia story (floor)
strada street
straniero foreign
strano[a] strange (odd)
stretto narrow
stretto tight
studente student
stupido[a] stupid
stuzzicadenti toothpick
su on
su up
subito soon
succhiotto pacifier
succo juice
sud south
sudare sweat (v)

suocera mother-in-law
supermercato supermarket
supplemento supplement
sveglia alarm clock
svegliarsi wake up
Svizzera Switzerland

T

taglia size
tagliaunghie nail clipper
taglio di capelli haircut
tappeto carpet
tappeto rug
tappi per le orecchie earplugs
tappo cork
tardi late
tasca pocket
tasse tax
tavolo table
tazza cup
teatro play
teatro theater
telefono telephone
televisione television
temperatura temperature
tempo weather
temporale storm
tenda tent
tenere keep
tenero tender
tennis tennis
termometro thermometer
terra earth
terribile terrible
testa head

tetto   roof
tiepido   lukewarm
timido[a]   shy
tirare   pull
tirare   throw
toilette   toilet
torcia   flashlight
torre   tower
tossire   cough (v)
totale   total
tradizionale   traditional
tradurre   translate
traffico   traffic
traghetto   ferry
tramonto   sunset
tranquillo   quiet
traveler's check   traveler's check
treno   train
triste   sad
troppo   too
tu   you (informal)
tunnel   tunnel
turista   tourist
tutto   everything

U

ubriaco   drunk
uccello   bird
uccidere   kill
udire   hear
ufficio   office
ultimo   last
un altro   another
una volta   once
università   university

uomini   men
uomo   man
urgente   urgent
usare   use
uscita   exit

V

valigia   suitcase
valle   valley
vasca da bagno   bathtub
vecchio[a]   old
vedere   see
vedova   widow
vedovo   widower
vegetariano[a]   vegetarian (n)
vela   sailing
velocità   speed
vendere   sell
venerdì   Friday
venire   come
vento   wind
verde   green
vestiti   clothes
vestito   dress (n)
via aerea   air mail
viaggiare   travel
viaggio   journey
viaggio   trip
vicino   near
video   video
video camera   video camera
video registratore   video recorder
vietato   forbidden
vietato fumare   non-smoking

DICTIONARY

vigneto vineyard
villaggio village
vino wine
viola purple
violenza carnale rape (n)
virus virus
visita visit (n)
visitare visit (v)
vista view
vita life
vita waist
vitamine vitamins
vivere live (v)
voce voice
volare fly
volere want
volo flight
vomitare vomit (v)
vuoto empty

Z

zainetto backpack
zaino rucksack
zanzara mosquito
zero zero
zia aunt
zio uncle
zoo zoo

Hurdling the Language Barrier

Don't be afraid to communicate

Even the best phrase book won't satisfy your needs in every situation. To really hurdle the language barrier, you need to leap beyond the printed page, and dive into contact with the locals. Never allow your lack of foreign language skills to isolate you from the people and cultures you traveled halfway around the world to experience. Remember that in every country you visit, you're surrounded by expert, native-speaking tutors. Spend bus and train rides letting them teach you.

Start conversations by asking politely in the local language, "Do you speak English?" When you speak English with someone from another country, talk slowly, clearly, and with carefully chosen words. Use what the Voice of America calls "simple English." You're talking to people who are wishing it was written down, hoping to see each letter as it tumbles out of your mouth. Pronounce each letter, avoiding all contractions and slang. For bad examples, listen to other tourists.

Keep things caveman-simple. Make single nouns work as entire sentences ("Photo?"). Use internationally-understood words ("Self-service" works in Sicily). Butcher the language if you must. The important thing is to make the effort. To get air mail stamps, you can flap your wings and say "tweet, tweet." If you want milk, moo and pull two imaginary udders. Risk looking like a fool.

If you're short on words, make your picnic a potluck. Pull

APPENDIX

out a map and point out your journey. Draw what you mean. Bring photos from home and introduce your family. Play cards or toss a Frisbee. Fold an origami bird for kids or dazzle 'em with sleight-of-hand magic.

Go ahead and make educated guesses. Many situations are easy-to-fake multiple choice questions. Practice. Read timetables, concert posters and newspaper headlines. Listen to each language on a multilingual tour. Be melodramatic. Exaggerate the local accent. Self-consciousness is the deadliest communication-killer.

Choose multilingual people to communicate with, like students, business people, urbanites, young well-dressed people, or anyone in the tourist trade. Use a small note pad to keep track of handy phrases you pick up—and to help you communicate more clearly with the locals by scribbling down numbers, maps, and so on. Some travelers carry important messages written on a small card: vegetarian, boiled water, your finest ice cream.

Numbers and Stumblers:

■ Europeans write a few numbers differently than we do. The one has an upswing (1), the four looks like a lightning bolt (4), and the seven has a cross (7).

■ Europeans write the date in this order: day/month/year. Christmas is 25-12-01, not 12-25-01.

■ Commas are decimal points and decimals are commas. A dollar and a half is 1,50 and 5.280 feet are in a mile.

■ The European "first floor" isn't the ground floor, but the first floor up.

■ When counting with your fingers, start with your thumb. If you hold up only your first finger, you'll probably get two of something.

International words

As our world shrinks, more and more words hop across their linguistic boundaries and become international. Savvy travelers develop a knack for choosing words most likely to be universally understood ("auto" instead of "car," "kaput" rather than "broken," "photo," not "picture"). Internationalize your pronunciation. "University," if you play around with its sound (oo-nee-vehr-see-tay), will be understood anywhere. Practice speaking English with a heavy Italian accent. Wave your arms a lot. Be creative.

Here are a few internationally understood words. Remember, cut out the Yankee accent and give each word an Italian sound.

Stop	Kaput	Vino	Restaurant
Ciao	Bank	Hotel	Bye-bye
Rock 'n roll	Post	Camping	OK
Auto	Picnic	Amigo	Autobus (boos)
Nuclear	Macho	Tourist	English
Yankee	Americano	Mama mia	Michelangelo
Beer	Oo la la	Coffee	Casanova (romantic)
Chocolate	Moment	Sexy	Disneyland
Tea	Coca-Cola	No problem	Passport
Telephone	Photo	Photocopy	Police
Europa	Self-service	Toilet	Information
Super	Taxi	Central	Rambo

Let's Talk Telephones

Smart travelers use the telephone every day to check on tourist information, call home, or make hotel reservations. If there's a language problem, ask someone at your hotel to talk to your next hotel for you.

The card-operated public phones are easier to use than coin-operated phones. Buy a *carta telefonica* (telephone card) at post offices, *tabacchi* (tobacco shops), or machines near phone booths (some phone booths indicate where the nearest phone card sales outlet is located). Your *carta telefonica* will work for local, long distance, and international calls made from card-operated public phones throughout Italy. Before using your card, tear off the perforated corner. Dial patiently, as if the phone doesn't understand numbers very well.

Hotel room phones can be reasonable for local calls, but a terrible rip-off for long-distance calls. To avoid hassles, make your calls from a phone booth, the post office, or a metered phone at a bar.

European time is six/nine hours ahead of the east/west coast of the United States. Breakfast in Venice is midnight in California.

Dialing Direct

Calling Between Countries: First dial the international access code (00 if you're calling from Europe, 011 if you're calling from the USA or Canada), the country code of the country you're calling, the area code (if it it starts with zero, you generally drop the zero—but keep the zero if you're calling Italy), and then the local number. See international access codes and country codes below.

Specifics on calls between Italy and the U.S.A.: To call the U.S.A. from Italy, dial 00-1-area code-local number. To call Italy from the USA, dial 011-39-local number.

Calling Long Distance Within Most European Countries (but not Italy): First dial the area code (including its zero), then the local number.

Calling Long Distance Within Italy: Italy doesn't use area codes. Simply dial the local number in its entirety, whether you're calling across the country or across the street.

Europe's Exceptions: Some countries do not use area codes, such as Italy, Spain, Portugal, France, Norway, Denmark, Belgium and Switzerland. To make long-distance calls within any of these countries, just dial the local number. To make an international call to Italy, Spain, Portugal, Norway or Denmark, dial the international access code, the country code, and then the local number in its entirety. To call France, Belgium or Switzerland, dial the international access code, the country code, then the local number *without* its initial zero.

International Access Codes

When dialing direct, first dial the international access code of the country you're calling from. For the USA and Canada it's 011. Virtually all other European countries use "00" as their international code; the only exceptions are Finland (990) and Lithuania (810).

Country Codes

After dialing the international access code, dial the code of the country you're calling.

Austria—43	France—33	Netherlands—31
Belgium—32	Germany—49	Norway—47
Britain—44	Greece—30	Portugal—351
Czech Rep.—420	Ireland—353	Spain—34
Denmark—45	Italy—39	Sweden—46
Estonia—372	Latvia—371	Switzerland—41
Finland—358	Lithuania—370	U.S.A./Canada—1

ATT, MCI, & SPRINT operators in Italy:

It's cheaper to call direct, but if you have a calling card and prefer to have an English-speaking operator dial for you, here are the numbers: ATT (172-1011), MCI (172-1022), and SPRINT (172-1877).

Weather

First line is average daily low (°F); second line average daily high (°F); third line, days of no rain.

	J	F	M	A	M	J	J	A	S	O	N	D
Rome	39	39	42	46	55	60	64	64	61	53	46	41
	54	56	62	68	74	82	88	88	83	73	63	56
	23	17	26	24	25	28	29	28	24	22	22	22

Your tear-out cheat sheet

Keep this sheet of the most essential Italian words and phrases in your pocket, so you can memorize them during idle moments, or quickly refer to them if you're caught without your phrase book.

English	Italian	Pronunciation
Good day.	**Buon giorno.**	bwohn **jor**-noh
Do you speak English?	**Parla inglese?**	**par**-lah een-**glay**-zay
Yes. / No.	**Sì. / No.**	see / noh
I don't speak Italian.	**Non parlo l'italiano.**	nohn **par**-loh lee-tah-leeah-noh
I'm sorry.	**Mi dispiace.**	mee dee-speeah-chay
Please.	**Per favore.**	pehr fah-**voh**-ray
Thank you.	**Grazie.**	graht-seeay
It's (not) a problem.	**(Non) c'è problema.**	(nohn) cheh proh-**blay**-mah
It's good.	**Va bene.**	vah **behn**-ay
You are very kind.	**Lei è molto gentile.**	lehee eh **mohl**-toh jayn-**tee**-lay
Goodbye!	**Arrivederci!**	ah-ree-vay-**dehr**-chee
Where is...?	**Dov'è...?**	doh-**veh**
...a hotel	**...un hotel**	oon oh-**tehl**
...a youth hostel	**...un ostello della gioventù**	oon oh-**stehl**-loh **dehl**-lah joh-vehn-**too**
...a restaurant	**...un ristorante**	oon ree-stoh-**rahn**-tay
...a supermarket	**...un supermercado**	oon soo-pehr-mehr-**kah**-doh
...a pharmacy	**...una farmacia**	**oo**-nah far-mah-**chee**-ah
...a bank	**...una banca**	**oo**-nah **bahn**-kah
...the train station	**...la stazione**	lah staht-seeoh-nay
...tourist information	**...informazioni per turisti**	een-for-maht-seeoh-nee pehr too-**ree**-stee
...the toilet	**...la toilette**	lah twah-**leht**-tay
men	**uomini, signori**	**woh**-mee-nee, seen-**yoh**-ree
women	**donne, signore**	**don**-nay, seen-**yoh**-ray

How much is it?	**Quanto costa?**	kwahn-toh **kos**-tah
Write it?	**Lo scrive?**	loh **skree**-vay
Cheap(er).	**(Più) economico.**	(pew) ay-koh-**noh**-mee-koh
Cheapest.	**Il più economico.**	eel pew ay-koh-**noh**-mee-koh
Is it free?	**È gratis?**	eh **grah**-tees
Is it included?	**È incluso?**	eh een-**kloo**-zoh
Do you have...?	**Ha...?**	ah
Where can I buy...?	**Dove posso comprare...?**	**doh**-vay **pos**-soh kohm-**prah**-ray
I would like...	**Vorrei....**	vor-**rehee**
We would like...	**Vorremo...**	vor-**ray**-moh
...this.	**...questo.**	**kweh**-stoh
...just a little.	**...un pochino.**	oon poh-**kee**-noh
...more.	**...di più.**	dee pew
...a ticket.	**...un biglietto.**	oon beel-**yay**-toh
...a room.	**...una camera.**	**oo**-nah **kah**-may-rah
...the bill.	**...il conto.**	eel **kohn**-toh
one	**uno**	**oo**-noh
two	**due**	**doo**-ay
three	**tre**	tray
four	**quattro**	**kwah**-troh
five	**cinque**	**cheeng**-kway
six	**sei**	**se**hee
seven	**sette**	**seht**-tay
eight	**otto**	**ot**-toh
nine	**nove**	**nov**-ay
ten	**dieci**	dee**ay**-chee
hundred	**cento**	**chehn**-toh
thousand	**mille**	**mee**-lay
At what time?	**A che ora?**	ah kay **oh**-rah
Just a moment.	**Un momento.**	oon moh-**mayn**-toh
Now.	**Adesso.**	ah-**dehs**-soh
soon / later	**presto / tardi**	**prehs**-toh / **tar**-dee
today / tomorrow	**oggi / domani**	**oh**-jee / doh-**mah**-nee

What we do at Rick Steves' Europe Through the Back Door

At ETBD we value travel as a powerful way to better understand and contribute to the world in which we live. Our mission at ETBD is to equip travelers with the confidence and skills necessary to travel through Europe independently, economically, and in a way that is culturally broadening. To accomplish this, we:

- Teach budget European travel skills seminars;
- Research and write guidebooks to Europe;
- Write and host a public television series;
- Sell European railpasses, our favorite guidebooks, travel videos, bags, and accessories;
- Provide European travel consulting services;
- Organize and lead free-spirited, no-grumps, small-group tours of Europe;
- Sponsor our European Travel Resource Center near Seattle, and our Web site at www.ricksteves.com

...and we travel a lot.

Rick Steves' tours

If you like our independent travel philosophy but would like to benefit from the camaraderie and efficiency of group travel, our European tours may be right up your alley. Every year we lead friendly, intimate tours through Western Europe, Eastern Europe, France, Italy, Britain, Ireland, Germany-Austria-Switzerland, Spain-Portugal, Scandinavia, and Turkey — plus week-long getaways to London, Paris, Rome, Venice, Florence and Prague. For details, call 425/ 771-8303 ext. 217, or visit www.ricksteves.com and ask for our free tour booklet.

on packing, itinerary-planning, transportation, finding rooms, travel photography, keeping safe and healthy, plus chapters on Rick's favorite back door discoveries.

Mona Winks: Self-Guided Tours of Europe's Top Museums

Let's face it, museums can ruin a good vacation. But *Mona* takes you by the hand, giving you fun and easy-to-follow self-guided tours through Europe's 20 most frightening and exhausting museums and cultural obligations. Packed with more than 200 maps and illustrations.

Europe 101: History and Art for the Traveler

A lively, entertaining crash course in European history and art, *Europe 101* is the perfect way to prepare yourself for the rich cultural smorgasbord that awaits you.

Rick Steves' Postcards from Europe

For twenty-five years Rick Steves has been exploring Europe, sharing his tricks and discoveries in guidebooks and on TV. Now, in *Postcards from Europe* he shares his favorite personal travel stories and his off-beat European friends – all told in that funny, down-to-earth style that makes Rick his Mom's favorite guidebook writer.

Rick Steves' European Phrase Books: French, Italian, German, Spanish/Portuguese, and French/Italian/German (3-in-1)

Finally, a series of phrase books written especially for the budget traveler! Each book gives you the words and phrases you need to communicate with the locals about room-finding, food, health and transportation—all spiced with Rick Steves' travel tips, and his unique blend of down-to-earth practicality and humor.

Faxing your hotel reservation

Most hotel managers know basic "hotel English." Photocopy and enlarge this form, then fax away.

. . . .

One page fax   My fax #:_____

To: Today's date: ____ / ____ / ____

From: day   month   year

Dear Hotel _____,

    Please make this reservation for me:

Name: _____

Total # of people: ____   # of rooms: ____   # of nights: ____

Arriving: ____ / ____ / ____   Time of arrival (24 hour olook): _____
       day   month   year   (I will telephone if later)

Departing: ____ / ____ / ____
         day   month   year

Room(s):   Single   Double   Twin   Triple   Quad   Quint
With: Toilet Shower   Bathtub   Sink only
Special needs: View   Quiet   Cheapest room   Ground floor

Credit card: Visa   Mastercard   American Express

Card #: _____   Exp. date: _____

Name on card: _____

If a deposit is necessary, you may charge me for the first night. Please fax or mail me confirmation of my reservation, along with the type of room reserved, the price, and whether the price includes breakfast. Thank you.

Signature: _____

Name: _____

Address :_____

Phone: _____   E-mail: _____

More books by Rick Steves...

*Now more than ever, travelers are determined to get the most out of every mile, minute and dollar. That's what Rick's books are all about. He'll help you have a better trip **because** you're on a budget, not in spite of it. Each of these books is published by Avalon Travel Publications, and is available through your local bookstore, or through Rick's free travel newsletter.*

Rick Steves' Italy

For a successful trip, raw information isn't enough. In his country and city guides, Rick weeds through each region's endless possibilities to give you candid, straight-forward advice on what to see, where to sleep, how to get the most out of every day and dollar. Besides Italy, the series includes....

Rick Steves' Rome
Rick Steves' Venice
Rick Steves' Florence
Rick Steves' Best of Europe
Rick Steves' France, Belgium & the Netherlands
Rick Steves' Paris
Rick Steves' Germany, Austria & Switzerland
            (with Prague)
Rick Steves' Great Britain
Rick Steves' London
Rick Steves' Ireland
Rick Steves' Scandinavia
Rick Steves' Spain & Portugal

Rick Steves' Europe Through The Back Door

Updated every year, *ETBD* has given thousands of people the skills and confidence they needed to travel through the less-touristed "back doors" of Europe. You'll find chapters

Rick Steves'
ITALY

A Tour Guide in Your Pocket!

This guidebook is all you'll need—there's a comfortable mix of grande *cities,* tranquillo *towns, and colorful Riviera villages.*

Rick Steves' Italy *includes:*

- The best sights and activities
- Friendly places to eat and sleep—heavy on character, light on the budget
- Suggested day plans and trip itineraries mixing famous sights with little-known discoveries
- Clear transportation Instructions to guide you smoothly from point to point by car or train
- Dozens of custom-designed, user-friendly maps

AVALON TRAVEL

Rick Steves' books are available at your local bookstore.

To get Rick's free newsletter and learn more about Europe the Back Door, call (425) 771-8303 or visit www.ricksteves.com.

www.ricksteves.com

Rick Steves' popular Web site is sure to raise your European travel I.Q. You'll find a user-friendly online version of Rick's Guide to European Railpasses, a Graffiti Wall filled with advice from traveling readers, late-breaking book updates, and more. You can even sign up to get Rick's free monthly e-mail newsletter!

Tell me what you think

Your feedback will do a lot to improve future editions of this phrase book. To help tomorrow's travelers travel smarter, please jot down any ideas, phrases, and suggestions as they hit you during your travels, and then send them to me. Mille grazie!

Rick Steves' Europe Through the Back Door

130 Fourth Ave. N
PO Box 2009
Edmonds, WA 98020
rick@ricksteves.com